MORE MANDY'S

more recipes we love

MORE MANDY'S

more recipes we love

By Mandy Wolfe, Rebecca Wolfe and Meredith Erickson

appetite
by RANDOM HOUSE

Appetite by Random House® and colophon are registered trademarks of Penguin Random House LLC.

Library and Archives of Canada Cataloguing in Publication is available upon request.
ISBN: 978-0-525-61049-6
eBook ISBN: 978-0-525-61050-2

Photography by Alison Slattery, Two Food Photographers
Design by Cow Goes Moo
Illustrations by Neethi
Printed in China

Published in Canada by Appetite by Random House®, a division of Penguin Random House Canada Limited

www.penguinrandomhouse.ca

10   9   8   7   6   5   4   3   2   1

To our mom, Judy Wolfe, aka Joodles. When we weren't sure this dream of ours could fly, you gave us our wings. Thank you for showing us how to love unconditionally, wholeheartedly, and effortlessly. You always said one day we would understand, and we can now proudly say we really do. We love you. Thank you.

Contents

Where We Are Now

We're baaaaaaack!

First things first: thank you to everyone who bought our first cookbook *Mandy's Gourmet Salads: Recipes for Lettuce and Life*. We have been completely overwhelmed by the response and have loved seeing all the Mandy's salads being made at home across Canada and beyond. It's been both humbling and completely inspiring, and that's why we wanted to give you more salad recipes, more dressings, more sweets . . . more Mandy's!

Our first book was all about our signature salads, the menu mainstays since our opening day in the early 2000s. And now that you have the essentials, we're giving you (a lot) more recipes so you can kick your salad game up a notch. In this book you'll find two main themes. The first, as you may have guessed from the cover, is fall. Our first book was published in summer, so for this one we really want to focus on celebrating seasonal goodness from September until May . . . which, yes, makes up most of the Canadian calendar year. It's all about bringing you brightness, hits of citrus and veg, and inspiration for pantry creativity in those colder months, when we tend to all run a bit low. This is also why we're bringing you close to 20 soup recipes too, to keep you healthy—and not reaching for the same pre-packaged boxes from the freezer night after night.

Our second theme is international flavors. Increased international flavors are something we've been progressively showcasing in our monthly salads. Each month we aim to come up with a new recipe and a way to bring new flavor combos to the menu. For inspiration, we rely on our past travels, our city of Montreal, and brainstorming with our staff. This is one of the best parts of our job, as we get to explore our local community grocery stores, find traditional ingredients that are new to us, and then wax poetic about them on our menu. We're loving our Island Chicken Salad, for example (page 95), Jerk-Spiced Shrimp Salad (page 97), and Spicy Kani Salad (page 109), and we hope you do too. The Island Rice and Beans (page 96) recipe alone was our recipe tester Kendra's favorite discovery. It's wildly addictive! Which brings us to another point: more so than in the first book, you'll find a lot of salad additions in this book that work as standalone dishes. The Satay Mock Chicken (page 118), Pikliz (page 123), Ras el Hanout Vegan Crumble (page 119), Ba-corn (page 124) . . . these are all additions to salads that also work great on their own.

A rule of thumb as you use this book . . . There really are no rules! The suggested salad and dressing combinations on the following pages (and that we sell in our shops) are simply that: suggestions. You're always welcome to customize and mix and match when you come to one of our salad bars, and obviously that goes for in your home too. Enjoy!

XO Mandy + Becca
Fall 2022

Travel

Traveling was an integral part of our upbringing. And it's where we both derive so much of our creativity . . . for Mandy with food and for Rebecca with design.

We were very lucky that our parents took us to beautiful far reaches of the globe as children and as teenagers. They taught us the invaluable and immeasurable richness of encountering different people everywhere we went, and learning words from new languages like Swahili, or trying different foods like spicy jerk chicken off the back roads of the South Coast of Jamaica. This passion and curiosity have led us to more travels as adults and a keen appreciation for trips whenever we can take them. A word to the young—travel while you can, see as many places as possible, talk to people who are different from you, and, an absolute must: eat the food of the locals, wherever you go!

Mandy spent a great deal of time in Southeast Asia in her twenties—a big trip after college to Thailand, Laos, Cambodia, and Vietnam—which inspired so many of her culinary tendencies. Her love of everything European and Central and South American is also apparent in her recipes. The Mandy's menu is an eclectic mix of her favorite ingredients and combinations inspired by each culture's food repertoire.

Rebecca's design aesthetic could be described as New England meets Paris meets Palm Springs. Rebecca traveled every summer with our family to Kennebunkport on the coast of Maine, and the elegance of New England left its mark and shows itself in all of Mandy's dining rooms. Sitting in Parisian cafés and visiting the old villages of Tuscany also laid a design groundwork with the influence of old-school European sophistication. Most recently, Rebecca's biggest inspiration has come from a tiny little speck in the Bahamas called Harbour Island. The combination of its retro glamour, colorful architecture, and magnificent natural beauty has been unforgettable. She still travels there regularly and always comes home more inspired than when she left. The local interior designer, India Hicks, was an inspiration before Rebecca ever visited Harbour Island, and still is. India's use of texture and color, incorporating the natural elements of the island into everything from her table settings to her wall decor, sparked a lot of inspiration. For all of the Mandy's interiors, Rebecca has pulled from the design concepts she has experienced on her travels, adding her own spin on them as she goes.

A Note on Music

Growing up, music was a huge part of our world. Whether it was blaring from our parents' radio around the house, or from the cassette player in our wood-paneled Grand Wagoneer on the long drive to the country every weekend, we lived and breathed music. We used to hit "play and record" on our tape players at home when we heard our favorite new song come on radio stations like Mix 96 or CHOM FM—if you know, you know! Both our parents had a natural affinity for good tunes, our mom more with rock and artists like Elvis and the Beatles, and our father more with rhythm and blues, playing the whole spectrum of doo-wop from its earliest artists like Frankie Lymon and the Platters to more recent Kool and the Gang. To this day, listening to R&B reminds us of our dad.

Every member of the Rat Pack was a household name for us, and we fell in love with jazz, funk, and above all, Motown. If we had to pick one genre that is the root of all our music love, it would definitely be Motown. Marvin Gaye, the Jackson 5, the Temptations, the Supremes, Stevie Wonder, you name it. We not only knew it; it was the soundtrack to our childhood.

As we grew up and emerged as our own people, all this music from our childhoods created an intense commitment in us to keep music a huge part of our lives—and of our children's lives, and in the spirit of our restaurants. We both lean more toward upbeat rhythms; we fell deeply in love with the likes of 60's rocksteady reggae, then got into the more mainstream reggae of the 70s & 80s. We also love disco, hip-hop, early rap, rock, folk, house, electronic, dance . . . Really, we love it all! We're both fanatics about dancing in our living rooms and kitchens, and we both love curating our favorite playlists—which might be what we'd do all day if we weren't making salads.

Scan here for a couple of our favorite playlists:

Our Salads

The salads in this book have some new, even bolder, flavors and ingredients than those in our first book, but how we come up with these recipes (and our belief about what makes a good one) hasn't changed since our very first salad counter. A lot of what you read in our first book still holds true, so we've adding some of that key info here again for you to read through.

To remind you: What sets Mandy's apart from all the other salad joints out there?

A lot. But mostly ratios and top quality everyyyything—plus very caring staff and the ambience of our locations. We're essentially a salad lab, one with weekly creative meetings where we try all the new flavor combinations of the season and also retest our current menu items. We're always thinking about ratios, both in the balance of our dressings and for our salads as a whole (i.e., no sogginess!).

It's really easy to f*#k up the ratio of a salad (too soggy, too much acid, too bitter), so getting it right is something we spend a lot of time on. Our general rules? Well, texturally, we like to make sure there are equal parts creaminess (avocado in almost every salad, or a nice soft cheese!), crunchiness (pita, tortilla, toasted nuts or seeds, or a crunchy vegetable), tartness—either from citrus (lemon or lime) in the salad dressing or tangy fruit in the salad (pomegranate seeds, pear, apple, cranberries)—and always—always—fat (olive oil, mayonnaise, egg, cheese, nuts, or, yes, avocado again).

Our flavor combinations may be globally inspired, but whenever we can, we use local and organic ingredients (almost always). We've included a list of local farms we love on page 59 and encourage you to seek out what's best in your area. If you're in Canada and having trouble finding fresh produce, contact us. For real—find us on Instagram or email us, and we'll look into your best local purveyors.

As this book is more fall and winter in focus, you'll notice we use fewer tomatoes and fresh berries in our recipes, but we ramp (no pun intended!) it up on pears, apples, pumpkin, sweet potatoes, kale, and of course root vegetables like beets, squash, leeks, garlic, and fennel. And we also use local grains and seeds in our salads and soups to keep us going through those –30°C (–22°F) Montreal months!

Your No-Fail Salad Equipment

A small blender for some of our favorite herby dressings

A salad spinner

A clean cutting board

A good knife

A large bowl for tossing:

we suggest metal bowls because you can bang them around without damaging them, but more importantly they don't stain or retain flavors from previous marinades or salad mixes

A squeeze bottle for dressing

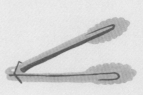
Your trusty tongs

MAKING MANDY'S SALADS AT HOME

We know that, with our first book in hand, you have become a seasoned salad pro. (Tongs? Check! Mixing bowl? Check! Knowing your favorite dressing recipe by heart? Check!) But we do hate to assume here at salad HQ, so here is a very brief review (or reminder!) of what you need to make Mandy's salads at home.

To get the most of this book, we suggest you start by making the salad recipes as we suggest them, with the dressings and toppings we recommend. Once you've tried a few, you'll get the hang of things, and then you can mix and match the salads with almost any other dressings or toppings you like. Customize!

Unless otherwise specified, each of the salad recipes is for one person to enjoy but can easily be scaled up to feed more. Making your own salads is all about organization and habit. Plan ahead, and just one hour a week can yield three salad dressings and enough chopping that you'll have a different salad for every lunch that week!

Oh, and please note that the salads in this book are organized according to the seasons, starting in early fall through winter into early spring, so you can flip through the pages accordingly.

NOTE ABOUT OUR DRESSINGS

Our salad dressings fit into one of two categories—dressings with fresh herbs, and dressings without. Those with fresh herbs usually make 1 cup and will be at their best for up to 3 days, refrigerated. Those without fresh herbs usually make 2 cups and will keep for up to 7 days, refrigerated.

The idea behind the yield of these recipes is that there should be enough dressing for 3 or 6 salads. At Mandy's we provide ⅓ cup (80 ml) of dressing for a takeout salad, but a salad should always be dressed to your personal preference.

NOTE ON MEASUREMENTS

We all know that eating well—both health-wise and joy-wise—is all about eating real food and keeping it heavy on the veggies, e.g., salads. What we're talking about here is healthy, fun, plentiful, and best of all, FLAVORFUL. So for the majority of our measurements, we use cups and tablespoons, as a more casual alternative to precise metric weights. That said, we're all about the ratios that lead to DELICIOUS, and so we have included metric measurements for our dressings—and for our desserts, because, well, baking is a whole other animal.

NOTE ON INGREDIENTS

Whenever possible we use local and organic ingredients and suggest you do too. As well, unless the recipe states otherwise, please assume:

- Eggs are extra large and freshly farmed
- Ginger and herbs are fresh (and remember . . . cilantro and parsley stems have a ton of flavor, so never omit them!)
- Meat is organic, or the best quality you can find
- Olive oil is extra virgin
- Salt is fine sea salt

More Than Salads!

There's no denying that we're best known for our gourmet salads, but there's so much more to Mandy's . . . and we really love to share it all! In our first book we shared some of our recipes for smoothies, grain bowls, and sweets; in this book we're sharing even more (because it is called *More Mandy's*, after all).

First up is morning fuel. Back during our first year of business at the Mandy's Old Port location, we served breakfast and brunch dishes too. Given that the neighborhood's demographic was mainly young working professionals, our guests wanted lighter chia seed parfaits (check!), smoothies (check!), and granola (check, right here!) to grab on their way to work; the more indulgent sit-down brunch options of, say, French toast, didn't pan out so well. We think there is a time and place for both—as does our sizable family—and we love flexing our morning muscles to make a hearty breakfast or brunch at home. Included in this chapter you'll find two options for avocado toast (pages 23 and 25), one of our favorite breakfast options. The versatility of an avocado shmear on a good bread (and the variety of options for dressing it up) knows no bounds, and these are just some kick-starter ideas. If you love any of our salad dressings, consider drizzling one (Smooth Sesame (page 136) or Épis-Style (page 149), perhaps?) over sliced avocado on a slice of crunchy toasted sprouted bread, then sprinkling with some sea salt and delicate fresh herbs, and you can thank us later.

We've also included a few new smoothies in this chapter, per the requests of fans of the smoothies from our first book. We've been selling our bottled salad dressings for a while now and, at the time of writing this, we have just started bottling our own fresh pressed juices too, which are flying off the shelves! Bottled smoothies are more challenging to produce, but we're working on it.

What else is new to this book? Soups! Montreal is an extreme-weather city with vastly different seasons, and the food at Mandy's really reflects that. Knowing our guests would be in search of warmth during the colder months, we added seasonal soups to our menu and everyone devoured them. For a while we were offering a "build your own soup" option with a variety of broths (chicken, veggie, and coconut milk) and inviting our guests to add their own ingredients, which would then be kind of blanched in the hot broth of their choice. It was fun while it lasted but eventually we scaled down our soup offerings to serve just the best of (what we think) is the best—and you'll find the recipes for those in this book, starting on page 156. We think simple, honest soup recipes are really underrated, and we hope you love the ones you find here—and love making them your own. When creating our soup recipes at home, feel free to customize per your taste and for the season. Our mom used to pimp a can of Campbell's Cream of Mushroom soup by adding shredded roasted chicken and serving it over steamed rice. Creating the Great Canadian Rice pilaf, perhaps?

And finally, in our sweets chapter we share more family recipes—even more than you'll find in the restaurants (so far!)—which are collection of homey Canadiana desserts that speak to all generations. In there are throwbacks to our family's ancestors in England, with Earl Grey Pound Cake (page 203) and Nana's "Chew" (page 212) that our grandma made for decades, and brownies we know the kids in your life will devour (page 219). If you have even a fraction of the sweet tooth that Mandy does, you'll love the supreme comfort and sweet satisfaction our sweets recipes offer.

Morning Fuel

★ CHAPTER ONE ★

Nutty Crunchy Granola

∘ MAKES 6 CUPS ∘

This granola recipe does not have the usual rolled oats as a main ingredient. Instead, it's all about puffed quinoa (which helps to aerate some of the otherwise dense volume), pecans, and seeds. The coconut oil gives it a little tropical moisture, and the almond butter coats everything with a delicious sweetness, almost like a salted caramel sauce, but healthier. This recipe is gluten-free.

INGREDIENTS

- 1 cup shredded unsweetened coconut
- ¾ cup puffed quinoa
- 1¼ cups pecans, coarsely chopped
- ¾ cup pumpkin seeds
- ⅓ cup black sesame seeds
- ⅓ cup white sesame seeds
- ½ cup agave syrup
- ½ cup almond butter
- ¼ cup coconut oil
- 2 teaspoons vanilla extract
- 2 teaspoons salt

DIRECTIONS

Preheat the oven to 350°F.

In a large bowl, mix the shredded coconut, puffed quinoa, pecans, pumpkin seeds, and both sesame seeds together.

In a small heavy-bottomed saucepan over medium-low heat, warm the agave syrup, almond butter, coconut oil, vanilla, and salt, whisking until smooth and homogeneous, then remove from the heat.

Pour the almond-butter sauce into the coconut mixture and use a spatula or wooden spoon to stir until all the ingredients are evenly coated.

Line a sheet tray with parchment paper and spread the granola over it. Bake for 10 to 15 minutes, stirring 2 or 3 times along the way, until dry and golden brown (it can turn dark brown quickly, so be watchful!).

Remove the granola from the oven and allow to cool to room temperature before using your hands to break up the mixture into bite-size pieces and transferring to an airtight storage container. This granola will keep, at room temperature, for up to 10 days.

Maple Cinnamon Granola

∘ MAKES 6 CUPS ∘

This granola is chewier and stickier than the previous granola recipe.
With the rolled oats, maple syrup, seeds, and brown sugar, it has the
chew and mouthfeel of a homemade granola bar. It's the recipe we
often make for our Mandy's staff, as it's not only great for breakfast
but perfect for a quick afternoon pick-me-up snack too.

INGREDIENTS

- 1½ cups rolled oats
- 1 cup puffed quinoa
- 1 cup sunflower seeds
- ½ cup pumpkin seeds
- ⅓ cup black and white sesame seeds
- ½ cup avocado oil
- ½ cup maple syrup
- ⅓ cup lightly packed brown sugar
- 1½ teaspoons ground cinnamon
- 1½ teaspoons salt
- 2 teaspoons vanilla extract

DIRECTIONS

Preheat the oven to 350°F.

In a large bowl, combine the rolled oats, puffed quinoa, sunflower seeds, pumpkin seeds, and sesame seeds, stirring to distribute.

In a small heavy-bottomed saucepan, combine the avocado oil, maple syrup, brown sugar, cinnamon, salt, and vanilla. Whisk to combine over medium heat, stirring until the mixture is smooth and the sugar has dissolved, 5 to 6 minutes. Remove from the heat.

Line a sheet tray with parchment paper and spread the granola over it. Bake for 20 to 25 minutes, stirring 2 or 3 times along the way, until light golden brown.

Remove the granola from the oven and allow to cool to room temperature before using your hands or a spoon to break up the mixture and transferring to a storage container. This granola will keep, at room temperature, for up to 10 days.

Hummus Za'atar Toast

◦ SERVES 1 ◦

In the same way we like to highlight different cuisines through our salads, when we were serving brunch in our Old Montreal location we went through an international avocado toast phase, featuring flavors from around the globe. It was a lot of fun, and we never grew tired of creating (or eating) them. This one features our Middle Eastern inspired homemade hummus and zesty za'atar. Sahtein!

NOTE: AS A SNACK, THIS HUMMUS SPREAD RECIPE PAIRS PERFECTLY WITH OUR HOMEMADE GARLIC AND ROSEMARY PITA CHIPS (PAGE 130) #JUSTSAYING.

INGREDIENTS

- 1 or 2 fried eggs, per your appetite (optional)
- 1 slice thick-cut bread
- 2 tablespoons Hummus Spread (recipe below)
- ½ avocado
- 1 teaspoon za'atar

FOR OPTIONAL PIMPING OF YOUR TOAST, ADD ANY OF THE FOLLOWING:

- Ground sumac, sesame seeds, and chopped mint, parsley and thyme (1 to 2 teaspoons total)

DIRECTIONS

If you're going to add fried eggs to the toast, fry those now. Place the bread in your toaster and toast until golden brown.

While the bread is toasting, remove the half avocado from its shell in one piece. Slice finely but not all the way through. Evenly spread the hummus over the toast and fan out the avocado on top. Add the egg(s) and sprinkle with za'atar. Pimp your toast as desired.

HUMMUS SPREAD

MAKES 4 CUPS

INGREDIENTS

- 3½ cups canned chickpeas, drained and rinsed
- 1 teaspoon minced garlic
- ¼ cup olive oil
- ¾ cup lemon juice
- ½ cup tahini
- 2 teaspoons ground cumin
- 2 teaspoons salt
- ½ cup water

DIRECTIONS

Bring a medium pot of water to a boil. Add the chickpeas and cook until tender (2 to 3 minutes). Once tender, drain the chickpeas, but do not cool down.

Place the garlic and olive oil in a blender and process until you have a smooth paste. Add the warm chickpeas, lemon juice, tahini, cumin, and salt and blend until smooth, about 1 minute. Slowly add the water until you have a completely smooth paste. Adjust the seasoning to taste. The hummus will last refrigerated for up to 5 days.

Sun-Dried Tomato Avocado Toast

∘ SERVES 1 ∘

Our favorite Italian-inspired salad—lovingly called the Roma (recipe in our first book)—features sun-blasted tomatoes, fresh herbs like parsley and basil, and creamy bocconcini. That salad has taken on different versions of itself over the years, and, for breakfast, we wanted to turn those flavors into a tasty spread for a sun-drenched Italian-style avocado toast.

NOTE: THE CREAM CHEESE SPREAD YIELDS A LARGER AMOUNT THAN IS NEEDED IN THIS RECIPE, BUT THIS WILL LAST IN THE FRIDGE FOR 2 TO 3 WEEKS, BUT WE'RE PRETTY SURE YOU'LL FIND IT SO ADDICTIVE THAT WE GIVE IT MORE LIKE 1 WEEK, MAX.

INGREDIENTS

- 1 or 2 fried eggs, per your appetite (optional)
- 1 slice thick-cut bread (we love the 9-grain option from our local bakery, Hof Kelsten, but any grainy bread will do)
- ½ avocado
- 2 tablespoons Sun-Dried Tomato Cream Cheese (recipe below)
- Salt and freshly ground black pepper

DIRECTIONS

If you're going to add fried eggs to the toast, fry those now. Place the bread in your toaster and toast until golden brown.

While the bread is toasting, mash the avocado. Evenly spread the cream cheese over the toast and add the avocado on top. Add the egg(s) and season with salt and pepper.

SUN-DRIED TOMATO CREAM CHEESE

MAKES 3 CUPS

INGREDIENTS

- 2 cups full-fat cream cheese
- 1 cup full-fat sour cream
- ½ cup chopped scallions
- ¾ cup sun-dried tomatoes
- 1 cup basil leaves, torn
- 1 teaspoon salt
- 1 teaspoon freshly ground black pepper
- ¼ cup olive oil

DIRECTIONS

Soften the cream cheese at room temperature for 30 minutes before making the spread.

In a blender, place the cream cheese, sour cream, scallions, sun-dried tomatoes, basil leaves, and salt and pepper. Start to blend. Slowly drizzle the olive oil into the blender until the mixture becomes smooth. Adjust the seasoning to taste and place in an airtight container. This spread will last refrigerated for up to 3 weeks.

Almond Banana Toast

◦ SERVES 4 ◦

For many years, our favorite smoothie was the Rise and Shine (from cookbook number 1), as almond butter and berries are such a healthy and satisfying combo—and that smoothie specifically would carry us from 7 a.m., through our morning meetings, until 1 p.m. lunchtime. This toast is the Rise and Shine 2.0.

NOTE: PORTION-WISE WE DO 2 SLICES OF BREAD PER PERSON.

INGREDIENTS

- 8 thick-cut slices white or kamut or 9-grain bread
- 1 cup almond butter, room temperature
- 4 bananas
- 2 cups best-quality blueberries (optional)
- ¼ cup chia seeds
- Maple syrup, for drizzling
- Maldon salt flakes

DIRECTIONS

Slice the bread as close to serving time as possible. Place the bread in your toaster and toast until golden brown.

Spread the almond butter on the toast in a thick, even layer (about 2 tablespoons per slice). Peel and slice the bananas into rounds. Place the bananas on top of the almond butter.

Garnish each piece with blueberries, chia seeds, a drizzle of maple syrup, and a pinch of Maldon salt.

Buttery Challah French Toast

◦ SERVES 6 ◦

There is nothing that screams "weekend breakfast" more than French toast. Growing up, our mom, Joodles, would tout that one slice could be a savory meal (just add butter and salt), while another could be a dessert (maple syrup, sliced fruit). Always use challah bread. While some people prefer to fry their French toast in oil, we are proponents of LOTS of butter for that unmistakably rich and delicious crisp toastiness when it comes to fry time. This is best enjoyed with Quebec's pride and joy: a best-quality maple syrup. We use maple syrup from a family friend's production in Hatley Eastern Townships called Ferncliff. If that's not available where you are, St. Leon is also a great choice, as of course is the maple syrup from Au Pied de Cochon's Cabane à Sucre.

NOTE: PORTION-WISE, AIM FOR AT LEAST 2 SLICES PER PERSON!

INGREDIENTS

◦ 6 eggs
◦ ¼ cup whole milk
◦ ½ teaspoon vanilla extract
◦ 1 loaf challah bread, thickly sliced
◦ 2 tablespoons butter (at least)
◦ 2 cups maple syrup
◦ Salt (optional)
◦ 2 cups mixed berries (we do blueberries, blackberries, and strawberries)
◦ Confectioners' sugar, for sprinkling (optional)

DIRECTIONS

Place the eggs, milk, and vanilla in a large bowl and mix well with a whisk.

Once mixed, pour into a shallow, flat dish. Place the bread slices in the dish (only as many as you can fit in your frying pan) and allow to soak until evenly soaked through.

In a nonstick frying pan over medium-high heat, heat (but do not brown) some of the butter. Add the soaked bread slices to the pan, and gently move them side to side and cook for 1 to 2 minutes, then flip and cook for another 1 to 2 minutes on the other side. Repeat the soaking and frying with the remaining slices of bread. If the butter is leaving too many browned or burned bits, a quick wipe with a clean towel will bring your frying pan back to neutral, and ready for more butter.

Plate each slice of bread, pour maple syrup liberally over top, salt if you roll like that, and top with berries of your choice and a sprinkling of confectioners' sugar.

Mini Egg Bites

○ MAKES 1 DOZEN BITES (OR 2 DOZEN MINI BITES) ○

It's so hard to find a breakfast that's easily portable, not loaded with carbs and sugar, and ready in seconds (if you just reheat it). And so, voilà: Les Mini Egg Bites. You're baking muffin tins of these brekkie bombs, so you'll have lots to store in your fridge or freezer for the future when the mood strikes! The fun thing about these is that you can customize them to your liking—keeping them veggie (which these are) and mixing them up with different vegetables, or adding meat if you like. And they're great even if you're dairy-free—omit the cream and cheese and they'll be a little less fluffy but still taste delicious!

NOTE: PER YOUR PREFERENCE, YOU CAN USE A MINI MUFFIN TRAY OR REGULAR MUFFIN TRAY. THE COOKING TIMES ARE ADAPTED BELOW.

YOU WILL NEED

- 12-cup muffin tray or 24-cup mini muffin tray

INGREDIENTS

- ½ cup diced white onion
- 1 cup sliced button mushrooms
- 2 tablespoons olive oil
- 12 eggs
- ½ cup heavy cream
- ½ cup shredded cheddar
- ⅓ cup chopped sun-dried tomatoes
- 1 teaspoon shredded basil
- Salt and freshly ground black pepper

DIRECTIONS

Preheat the oven to 400°F.

Place the onion and mushrooms in a nonstick frying pan with the olive oil and cook over medium heat until soft. Remove from the heat and allow to cool.

Crack the eggs into a large bowl and whisk thoroughly. Add the cream, cheddar, sun-dried tomatoes, basil, and the onion and mushroom mixture, and mix well to combine. Season with salt and pepper.

Spray your chosen muffin tray with oil, then fill each cavity about three-quarters full with the egg mixture. Bake for 7 to 9 minutes for a mini muffin tray, and 15 minutes for a regular muffin tray. Keep an eye on these and do not overcook; they are ready when the eggs start to pull away from the sides of the molds and the tops look golden brown and caramelized.

Remove from the oven and allow to cool slightly. Eat right away, or refrigerate in an airtight container for up to 5 days. To reheat, simply pop in the microwave for 15 to 30 seconds.

Chia Seed Parfait

◦ SERVES 1 ◦

Around the same time as our breakfast egg bites (page 30) came into rotation, we were also making overnight chia seed parfaits at a couple of our locations. We tried selling them in 2016, but perhaps we were ahead of our time.

Chia seeds themselves don't pack a lot of flavor, so that's where your own personal additions, like your favorite nuts and berries, come in. Personally, we love this with our Nutty Crunchy Granola (page 20), blueberries, and pomegranate seeds.

NOTE: REGARDING YIELD, WE HAVE ONLY PROVIDED THE QUANTITIES FOR 1 CHIA SEED PARFAIT. YOU SHOULD MULTIPLY THE RECIPE ACCORDING TO YOUR DESIRE, BUT MOREOVER, THE AMOUNT OF ROOM YOU HAVE IN YOUR FRIDGE! BECAUSE KEEP IN MIND THAT THESE POTS NEED TO CHILL OVERNIGHT (TO ALLOW THE CHIA SEEDS TO PUFF UP) BEFORE YOU CAN ENJOY THEM IN THE MORNING. CHIA SEEDS ARE MIRACULOUS IN THAT THEY CAN ABSORB UP TO 12 TIMES THEIR WEIGHT IN LIQUID. THIS IS WHY THE NEXT DAY YOU DON'T JUST HAVE LIQUID MILK WITH CHIA SEEDS! THE SEEDS DEVELOP A COATING, AND THAT'S WHY CHIA-BASED DRINKS HAVE A GELATINOUS TEXTURE.

INGREDIENTS

- 1 cup milk of your choice (we love vanilla almond milk, but do whatever you like with cashew, oat, or—go crazy—full-fat dairy)
- 3 to 4 tablespoons whole chia seeds

TOPPING OPTIONS

- ¼ cup chopped fruit of your choice
- Unsweetened shredded coconut
- ¼ cup toasted nuts or Nutty Crunchy Granola (page 20)

DIRECTIONS

In a Mason jar, stir the milk and chia seeds together well. Set aside for 10 minutes, then stir again (otherwise you may find a Mason jar with clumps of seeds at the bottom and lots of unused liquid at the top). Cover and place in the fridge overnight to allow the chia seeds to puff up. In the morning, you will have perfectly consistent chia seed pudding. We like to layer the pudding with chopped fruit and shredded coconut, and sometimes almond butter (we love Maranatha Coconut Almond Butter, but use the nut butter of your choice), and then top it with granola. This parfait will last up to 5 days refrigerated.

Imperial Cheese Egg Scramble

◦ SERVES 4 ◦

MacLaren's Imperial Cheese is quintessential Canadiana, up there alongside politeness, beavertails, and feigning shock about the inevitable blizzard that hits Montreal at the end of every April (even though this weather phenomenon has occurred annually since the beginning of time). But what is this product in the little red-and-black tub in the dairy aisle?* In plain speech, it's spreadable ground sharp cheddar cheese that was created by dairyman Alexander MacLaren in southwestern Ontario in the 1890s. Now, while it's sold as a sort of artisanal cheese, let's not kid ourselves: it is indeed a Kraft processed product. And it is very, very delicious. We like it on celery, crackers, sausages, and burgers (meat- or vegetable-based), and in our scrambled eggs, like this recipe right here. It's especially comforting on those −15°C (5°F) April days.

INGREDIENTS

- 1 tablespoon salted or unsalted butter
- 8 eggs, room temperature
- ½ container of MacLaren's Imperial Cheese (so we're talking about 4½ ounces/125 g in weight)
- Salt and freshly ground black pepper

DIRECTIONS

In a medium saucepan over medium-high heat, melt the butter. Crack your eggs into a bowl but do not beat or whisk them. Leave them whole!

When the butter is bubbling, pour in the eggs and move them around verrrry gently with a spatula or wooden spoon, making sure not to crack the yolks. At the last minute, pierce the yolks so they ooze their yellow (almost orange if you're lucky with your egg farmer). Lower the heat and crumble the cheese over top. Let cook for about 20 seconds, then turn off the heat and combine the mixture with your spatula or wooden spoon. The eggs will still cook in the hot pan.

Crack some pepper on top, sprinkle with some salt, and serve with your favorite buttered toast. We love a good baguette for this one.

*Sorry, American friends, this product, at the time of publication, is still only available in Canada.

Fall Beetroot and Ginger Smoothie

◦ MAKES ONE 16-OUNCE SMOOTHIE ◦

Feeling the fall blahs? Needing an extra zing and pep in your step? You've got it here in our feel-good fall beetroot ginger smoothie, packed with extra nutrients and vitamins to keep you going. Beets (beetroot) are known to maintain heart health, control blood pressure, support brain function, aid digestion, reduce inflammation, reduce obesity risk, and increase energy levels. They have a low glycemic load, so they tend to be very diet friendly. Throw in some Quebec apples, carrots, kale, ginger, and lemon, and now we're talking!

INGREDIENTS

◦ 1 beet, stem removed, scrubbed and quartered
◦ 1 apple of your preference (we love Lobo or McIntosh variety), cored and quartered
◦ ½ cup finely chopped kale, rinsed and drained
◦ ¼ cup coarsely chopped carrot
◦ ¼ cup blueberries (fresh or frozen)
◦ 1 tablespoon finely chopped ginger (peeled or not, your choice)
◦ ½ cup ice cubes
◦ Juice of ½ lemon

DIRECTIONS

Add the beet, apple, kale, carrot, blueberries, ginger, ice, and lemon juice to your blender. Pulse for 5 to 8 seconds and then blend on medium for 20 to 30 seconds. Once smooth, pour into your smoothie cup and enjoy immediately.

Pumpkin Pie Smoothie

∘ MAKES ONE 16-OUNCE SMOOTHIE ∘

Have you, by any chance, looked through your pantry and noticed you went overboard buying pumpkin puree for those festive pumpkin pies? Us too. Use it here for the perfect fall morning or mid-afternoon pumpkin pie smoothie.

INGREDIENTS

- ½ cup 100% pure pumpkin puree
- ½ cup unsweetened vanilla-flavored almond, oat, or rice milk
- ½ frozen banana
- ½ tablespoon maple syrup
- ½ teaspoon pumpkin pie spice (we suggest Simply Organic brand)
- ½ teaspoon vanilla extract
- ¼ teaspoon salt
- 1 scoop (⅓ cup) vanilla protein powder (we love Bob's Red Mill Vanilla Protein Powder Nutritional Booster)
- Pecans, chopped, for garnish (optional)

DIRECTIONS

Add the pumpkin puree, almond milk, banana, maple syrup, pumpkin pie spice, vanilla, salt, and protein powder to your blender. Pulse for 5 to 8 seconds and then blend on medium for 20 to 30 seconds. Once smooth, pour into your smoothie cup. Garnish with the optional chopped pecans if you're feeling "extra," and enjoy immediately.

Tropical Creamsicle Smoothie

◦ MAKES ONE 16-OUNCE SMOOTHIE ◦

Do the gray days of early winter leave you craving some tropicalia? Us too. This smoothie is our spin on a popular smoothie choice at one of Montreal's beloved vegan restaurants, Aux Vivres, on St. Laurent Boulevard. It tastes of citrus and pineapple sherbet, but it's actually packed with vitamins, vegetables, and yes, good fat from coconut milk.

NOTE: THIS RECIPE IS ALSO DELICIOUS MIXED WITH GRANOLA (PAGE 20 AND 22) AND SERVED IN A BOWL RATHER THAN AS A SMOOTHIE.

INGREDIENTS

- ¼ cup orange juice, or a mix of ½ clementine and ½ orange juice
- ¼ cup carrot juice
- ½ avocado, chopped
- ½ cup chopped pineapple
- ¼ cup canned coconut milk (do not use the kind from the carton, it's too fluid— keep it canned only!)
- 1 tablespoon chopped ginger
- Mint leaves

DIRECTIONS

Add the orange juice, carrot juice, avocado, pineapple, coconut milk, ginger, and mint to your blender. Pulse for 5 to 8 seconds and then blend on medium for 20 to 30 seconds. Once smooth, pour into your smoothie cup and enjoy immediately.

Harvest Greens Smoothie

∘ MAKES ONE 16-OUNCE SMOOTHIE ∘

This smoothie is ace for digestive issues and perfect for those January detoxes. If you have any fruit lying around that is about to turn, do yourself a favor and chop those goodies up into small chunks and freeze them— especially pears and grapes—they'll be delicious in this smoothie.

INGREDIENTS

- 1 cup cashew or almond milk
- ½ cup frozen grapes
- ½ cup frozen pear chunks
- 1 banana
- ½ avocado
- 1 cup chopped lacinato kale or spinach
- ½ teaspoon ground cinnamon
- 1 tablespoon hemp hearts or flax seeds

DIRECTIONS

Add the cashew milk, grapes, pear chunks, banana, avocado, kale, cinnamon, and hemp hearts to your blender. Pulse for 5 to 8 seconds and then blend on medium for 20 to 30 seconds. Once smooth, pour into your smoothie cup and enjoy immediately.

Anti-Flu Hot Tonic

◦ SERVES 4 TO 6 ◦

Whenever we start feeling the shivers, aches, or fatigue of an oncoming cold, we turn to this tonic to help boost our immunity, as well as hydrate the crap out of ourselves; it's the ultimate pre-emptive, cold-fighting drink. The ingredients used to make it are readily found in most fridges, so it's quite easy to whip up a few quarts in no time. We put ours in a thermos and carry it with us while on the go.

INGREDIENTS

- 8 cups water
- 5 to 6 tablespoons ginger, peel on, washed and cut into thin rounds
- 2 lemons, washed and sliced into rounds
- 1 medium orange, washed and sliced into rounds
- 1 to 2 teaspoons cayenne (if you like it really spicy, you can definitely up the amount)
- 1 sprig rosemary
- 1 stick cinnamon, or 1 teaspoon ground cinnamon
- 2 tablespoons Quebec maple syrup
- 3 to 4 cloves garlic, smashed (if you're up for it and not afraid to smell a little pungent!)

DIRECTIONS

Place all the ingredients in a large pot over medium-high heat and bring to a boil. Lower the heat and simmer for 10 to 15 minutes. Using a sieve, strain out and discard the solids but preserve that liquid gold! If not using immediately, transfer to an airtight container and refrigerate for up to 3 days.

Puebla Hot Chocolate

∘ SERVES 4 ∘

An old friend of ours introduced us to a traditional way of preparing hot chocolate from their hometown of Puebla, Mexico, and helped us home in on an authentic version of this beloved warm drink. Mexican hot chocolate uses a wonderful "chocolate de metate," or stone-ground chocolate, pressed into bars called tablillas (tablets). You can find Mexican chocolate at most supermarkets—the two easiest to find brands are Abuelita by Nestlé and Ibarra. The real way to froth up this drink is using a molinillo (a traditional wooden whisk, often beautifully decorated); however, using a long, skinny whisk will also do the trick. If you feel like you want some extra fuego, feel free to sprinkle in some ancho chili powder at the end of your frothing.

NOTE: YOU CAN USE EITHER MILK OR WATER FOR THIS RECIPE. WITH MILK, IT WILL TASTE RICHER AND CREAMIER, AND WITH WATER, THE CHOCOLATE FLAVOR WILL BE MORE PRONOUNCED.

INGREDIENTS

- 4¼ cups whole milk or water (see note)
- 2 3-ounce bars of Mexican (drinking) chocolate such as Abuelita, coarsely chopped
- 1 tablespoon granulated sugar, for extra sweetness (optional)
- 4 cinnamon sticks, for garnish

DIRECTIONS

In a high-sided medium saucepan over medium-low heat, warm the milk, stirring occasionally, until it starts to steam, about 4 to 5 minutes. Add the chocolate and whisk until it is fully melted and incorporated.

Remove from the heat and use a molinillo or whisk to agitate the hot chocolate until the mixture turns creamy and very frothy, about 3 to 4 minutes (or you can cheat and blend the hot chocolate in a blender for 1 to 2 minutes). Taste and add a little sugar for extra sweetness, if desired. Serve hot, and garnish each cup with a cinnamon stick.

Salads

★ CHAPTER TWO ★

Satay Mock Chicken Salad

◦ SERVES 1 ◦

When we launched a limited night menu at our Old Port location in summer 2019, there was no doubt which dish was the most popular: our Peanut Satay Skewers. So, we did what we do best and turned the star of the show into a salad to enjoy during the daytime too.

The marinade used for the Satay Mock Chicken is the perfect blend of crunch, citrus tang, and peanut butter! Because we use mock chicken, the whole salad is vegan. However, the marinade can also be used with Roasted Chicken Breast (page 117), or it would be a nice complement to Seared Filet Mignon (page 120).

NOTE: DOMESTIC GODS AND GODDESSES, RECOMMENDED MARINATING TIME FOR THE PROTEIN IS 6 HOURS, AND YOU MAY ALSO NEED TO FACTOR IN TIME TO MAKE THE MOCK CHICKEN FIRST IF YOU DON'T HAVE ANY ON HAND. PLAN AHEAD!

INGREDIENTS

- 3 cups mesclun greens
- 1 cup chopped romaine lettuce
- ½ cup diced mango
- ¼ cup shredded red cabbage
- ¼ cup shredded carrots
- ¼ cup roasted salted peanuts, halved or crushed
- ½ cup crushed and toasted ramen noodles
- 2 tablespoons sliced scallions
- 2 tablespoons torn Thai basil leaves
- 2 tablespoons cilantro leaves and minced stems
- 2 tablespoons torn mint leaves
- ½ cup Satay Mock Chicken (page 118)

- ⅓ cup Satay Dressing (page 152)

DIRECTIONS

Combine all of the ingredients except for the Satay Mock Chicken in a large stainless-steel bowl. Top with the dressing and, using tongs, toss until well mixed and dressed. Transfer to a serving bowl and sprinkle the Satay Mock Chicken over top.

Summer Barbecue Salad

◦ SERVES 1 ◦

Canada is a country that loves and lives for fresh corn. As a riff on a classic Cobb salad, for this recipe we roasted corn with bacon lardons to create an extra crispy, fatty, sweet, salty delicious corn topping. Buy the best bacon you can and please just try to save it for the salad and not eat it by the forkful before you get to putting the salad together. This ba-corn "topping" would also be great served as a side at a last-gasp-of-summer barbecue, in which case we recommend you double the recipe.

INGREDIENTS

- 3 cups chopped iceberg lettuce
- 1 cup arugula
- ½ cup Ba-corn (page 124)
- ½ avocado, diced
- ¼ cup halved multicolored cherry tomatoes
- 2 tablespoons diced red onion
- 2 tablespoons flat-leaf parsley leaves
- 2 tablespoons minced chives

- ⅓ cup Blue Ranch 2.0 Dressing (page 137)

DIRECTIONS

Combine all of the ingredients in a large stainless-steel bowl. Top with the dressing and, using tongs, toss until well mixed and dressed.

Tuna Provençale Salad

◦ SERVES 1 ◦

We derive inspiration for our salads from every corner of the globe, and this salad is an ode to a memorable childhood late-summer trip to Provence with family friends. The way the French put together the saltiest and creamiest ingredients is divine, and this seared tuna salad is a perfect representation of that. If you don't have access to some fine fresh tuna, jarred tuna packed in olive oil will do the trick.

INGREDIENTS

- 3 cups chopped romaine
- ½ cup chopped radicchio
- ½ cup canned white kidney beans, drained and rinsed
- ¼ cup halved cherry tomatoes
- ¼ cup Niçoise olives, pitted
- ¼ cup Parmesan flakes
- 2 tablespoons diced or sliced red onion
- 2 tablespoons chopped dill fronds
- 2 tablespoons flat-leaf parsley leaves
- 1 hardboiled egg, quartered
- 1 portion Seared Tuna Fillet (page 122)

- ⅓ cup Niçoise Dressing (page 152)

DIRECTIONS

Combine all of the ingredients except for the Seared Tuna Fillet in a large stainless-steel bowl. Top with the dressing and, using tongs, toss until well mixed and dressed. Transfer to a serving bowl and arrange the seared tuna slices over top. Alternatively, you can toss the greens with the dressing, and layer the different components separately on a pretty plate as pictured here.

Feel Good Fall

○ SERVES 1 ○

Every October in Quebec, it's very easy to be inspired by all the autumn colors around us when we're dreaming up our monthly salads. In 2020, we created the Feel Good Fall salad, and it was a huge success: gorgeous roasted rainbow carrots with fennel seeds, candied pecans, creamy goat cheese, and a tangy pomegranate dressing. A delicious and harmonious autumn feast!

NOTE: YOU CAN FIND COOKED BEETS IN SOUS-VIDE PACKAGING AT YOUR LOCAL GROCER, TYPICALLY IN THE REFRIGERATED AISLE.

INGREDIENTS

- 3 cups mesclun greens
- 1 cup arugula
- ¼ cup cubed cooked beets
- ¼ cup crumbled goat cheese
- ¼ cup Fennel-Roasted Carrots (page 126)
- ¼ cup diced pear
- 2 tablespoons Candied Pecans (page 128)
- 2 tablespoons torn mint leaves

- ⅓ cup Pomegranate Dressing (page 140)

DIRECTIONS

Combine all of the ingredients in a large stainless-steel bowl. Top with the dressing and, using tongs, toss until well mixed and dressed.

Super Santé Salad

○ SERVES 1 ○

In 2017, we were approached to produce ready-made salads for resale at some of our local grocery stores. As you can imagine, there are a lot of rules and regulations around this scale of production. And, of course, we had to think of salads with ingredients that could stay extra fresh and not lose their luster or oxidize too quickly, so we got really creative and wholesome in the collection of ingredients we decided to use. We lovingly dubbed this salad the "Super Santé," aka "Super Healthy." It can be found in health food stores and organic grocers in and around Montreal, like Rachelle Béry.

INGREDIENTS

- 2 cups shredded curly kale
- 2 cups baby spinach
- ½ cup Roasted Marinated Tofu (page 119)
- ½ cup Roasted Sweet Potato (page 125)
- ¼ cup shredded carrots
- 2 tablespoons sunflower seeds
- 2 tablespoons dried cranberries

- ⅓ cup Very Berry Dressing (page 148)

DIRECTIONS

Combine all of the ingredients in a large stainless-steel bowl. Top with the dressing and, using tongs, toss until well mixed and dressed.

Canadian Farm Fresh

Shout-out here to one of our partners whom we love to work with whenever possible: Carya Farms. This local farm in Senneville, in the West Island (of Montreal), often supplies an organic field mix of lettuces and microgreens for our monthly special salads. Here is a brief address book of other farms that inspire us, and whom we encourage you to order your veggies from if you're in the Montreal area:

Juniper Farm

Lufa Farms

Ferme Pleine Lune

Agricola Cooperative Farm

Bluegrass Farm

Roots and Shoots Farm

Fermes aux Pleines Saveurs

Émile Peloquin

Spicy Corn Salad

◦ SERVES 1 ◦

On late-summer family road trips in Quebec, when we drove near the border with the US, there would be corn fields as far as the eye could see and roadside stands aplenty. You could stop at any farm for some freshly boiled corn, and the farmer would paint melted butter all over your ear of corn before handing it over. Heaven!

This salad takes corn and dresses it up with spices and a little heat to keep us going through the fall and winter months. With pineapple, jerk-spiced seasoning, and a creamy avocado dressing, this salad will lift you out of any winter doldrums and take you to a place where you can feel and taste the sun.

INGREDIENTS

- ¼ cup Long-Grain Rice (page 131)
- 3 cups chopped romaine lettuce
- 1 cup arugula
- ½ cup Roasted Jerk-Spiced Corn (page 126)
- ¼ cup diced pineapple
- ¼ cup diced cucumber
- ¼ cup halved cherry tomatoes
- 2 tablespoons Quick-Pickled Red Onion (page 123)
- 2 tablespoons cilantro leaves

- ⅓ cup Tropical Avocado Dressing (page 138)

DIRECTIONS

Combine all of the ingredients in a large stainless-steel bowl. Top with the dressing and, using tongs, toss until well mixed and dressed.

Rainbow Salad

○ SERVES 1 ○

Once upon a time, back in the early days of COVID-19, we tried to lift our spirits and boost immunity by creating this healthy vitamin-rich salad. You'll remember how the rainbow symbol swept the world, a global sign of optimism and hope in the face of great adversity. In Montreal, the rainbow was combined with the saying "Ça va bien aller!" or "Everything is going to be all right!" This salad is now a Mandy's mainstay, and a true edible pick-me-up.

INGREDIENTS

- 2 cups mesclun greens
- 1 cup radicchio
- 1 cup baby spinach leaves
- ¼ cup Parmesan Brussels Sprouts (page 126)
- ¼ cup shredded red cabbage
- ¼ cup diced red bell pepper
- ¼ cup shredded carrots
- ¼ cup diced red apple (we like Macintosh, Lobo, Honey Crisp, or Red Delicious)
- ¼ cup Roasted Sweet Potato (page 125)
- ¼ cup toasted walnuts

- ⅓ cup Sunshine Dressing (page 141)

DIRECTIONS

Combine all of the ingredients in a large stainless-steel bowl. Top with the dressing and, using tongs, toss until well mixed and dressed.

Roasted Leek Salad

∘ SERVES 1 ∘

We love leeks! They're onion's more subtle cousin, especially when you roast them with a little butter. We came up with this autumn salad as a showcase for Quebec's punchy McIntosh apples—a fall staple—and we paired the apple with a supporting duo of roasted fennel and leek, then kept things crunchy with toasted pecans and salty with ribbons of Parmesan, and then tossed it all up with a zesty lemon-thyme vinaigrette. This monthly salad was a huge hit, proving once again that good produce can easily be the star of any show.

INGREDIENTS

- ½ cup Quinoa (page 132)
- 1 cup mesclun greens
- 1 cup chopped romaine lettuce
- 1 cup arugula
- ½ cup chopped radicchio
- ¼ cup diced celery
- ¼ cup thinly sliced McIntosh apple
- ¼ cup halved grapes
- ¼ cup Roasted Fennel and Leek (page 124)
- ¼ cup Parmesan flakes
- 2 tablespoons pecan halves, toasted

- ⅓ cup Lemon Thyme Dressing (page 139)

DIRECTIONS

Combine all of the ingredients in a large stainless-steel bowl. Top with the dressing and, using tongs, toss until well mixed and dressed.

Keto 2.0 Salad

◦ SERVES 1 ◦

MANDY | The keto trend just won't quit! Speaking from personal experience, it can work for you if you work at it and stick to it. If you're a die-hard keto fan or having a keto fan over for lunch or dinner, file this one as a must-have salad; you won't feel deprived in the slightest with the bacon, blue cheese, salty olives, avocado, and decadent and creamy Parmesan Dressing!

INGREDIENTS

- 2 cups mesclun greens
- 1 cup chopped iceberg lettuce
- 1 cup chopped romaine lettuce
- ½ avocado, diced
- ¼ cup diced cucumber
- ¼ cup halved cherry tomatoes
- 2 tablespoons pitted Kalamata olives
- 2 tablespoons sliced red onion
- 2 slices bacon, cut into pieces and fried until crispy
- ¼ cup crumbled blue cheese
- 2 tablespoons torn tarragon leaves
- 2 tablespoons minced chives

- ⅓ cup Parmesan Dressing (page 142)

DIRECTIONS

Combine all of the ingredients in a large stainless-steel bowl. Top with the dressing and, using tongs, toss until well mixed and dressed.

Roasted Squash Salad

◦ SERVES 1 ◦

Autumn is squash and gourd heaven in Canada, and we're always looking for new ways to use this bountiful produce in our salads, where we roast and season them every which way. Lachlan McGillivray, head chef of Mandy's, suggested using almond butter in the dressing for this, in addition to the toasted walnuts in the salad. The end result is a nutty, creamy, heavenly autumn dish, perfect for lunch, or as dinner when paired with a steaming cup of soup.

NOTE: FIVE-SPICE POWDER IS A BLEND OF FIVE SPICES: CINNAMON, CLOVES, FENNEL SEED, STAR ANISE, AND SZECHUAN PEPPERCORN. IT IS A COMMON INGREDIENT IN CHINESE CUISINE, SAID TO FEATURE ALL FIVE BASIC TASTES: SWEET, SALTY, SOUR, BITTER, UMAMI. IT CAN BE FOUND IN ANY SPECIALTY SPICE SHOP AND MOST SUPERMARKETS.

INGREDIENTS

◦ 3 cups mesclun greens
◦ 1 cup chopped radicchio
◦ ½ cup diced Five-Spice Roasted Squash (page 124)
◦ ¼ cup sliced endive
◦ ¼ cup sliced pear
◦ 2 tablespoons chopped walnuts, toasted
◦ 2 tablespoons crumbled blue cheese
◦ ½ cup beet chips (we love the Hardbite ones)

◦ ⅓ cup Autumn Almond Dressing (page 140)

DIRECTIONS

Combine all of the ingredients in a large stainless-steel bowl. Top with the dressing and, using tongs, toss until well mixed and dressed.

Thanksgiving Salad

○ SERVES 1 ○

We realize that not everyone celebrates Thanksgiving, and that some people celebrate it solo. But that doesn't mean you have to miss out on the meal. And so we created this Thanksgiving-in-a-salad flavor. You have a couple of options here: this can BE your Thanksgiving dinner (turkey optional) or it can be a pimped salad to accompany your Thanksgiving dinner.

NOTE: YOU CAN FIND COOKED BEETS IN SOUS-VIDE PACKAGING AT YOUR LOCAL GROCER, TYPICALLY IN THE REFRIGERATED AISLE.

INGREDIENTS

- 2 cups chopped romaine lettuce
- 1 cup mesclun greens
- ¼ cup diced cooked beets
- ¼ cup shredded carrots
- ¼ cup Roasted Sweet Potato (page 125)
- ¼ cup crumbled goat cheese
- ¼ cup Crispy Fried Shallots (page 129)
- 2 tablespoons dried cranberries
- 2 tablespoons toasted walnuts, coarsely chopped
- 2 tablespoons chopped flat-leaf parsley leaves
- 1 cup shredded cooked turkey (optional)

- ⅓ cup Sage and Rosemary Dressing (page 142)

DIRECTIONS

Combine all of the ingredients in a large stainless-steel bowl. Top with the dressing and, using tongs, toss until well mixed and dressed.

Spicy Eggplant Salad

◦ SERVES 1 ◦

MANDY | In my Montreal student days, I would hop on the metro at least three times a week to get to the Faubourg Ste-Catherine mall downtown and a tucked-away Thai food stand called Cuisine Bangkok: it was me and a consistent lineup of die-hard Thai food lovers. You could tell the cooks how spicy you liked things, and they'd mark it on your order: "X" was mild, "XX" was hot, and "XXX" was Thai hot . . . My absolute favorite was the spicy eggplant with Thai basil, served with a steaming bowl of jasmine rice. Twenty years later, I turned the memory of it into a monthly special in honor of Cuisine Bangkok, which had by then relocated to Ste-Catherine Street East, in the Village. Here is the salad version. Sidenote: they have since reopened in the Faubourg food court under the name "Mamma Bangkok." Their food is still as tasty as I remember.

NOTE: THIS RECIPE REQUIRES SOME PREP WORK—MAKING THE SPICY BASIL EGGPLANT, THE JASMINE RICE, AND THE CRISPY FRIED SHALLOTS AHEAD OF TIME (THOUGH YOU CAN BUY FRIED SHALLOTS AT ANY ASIAN GROCERY STORE). WE PROMISE YOU THE EFFORT IS WORTH IT FOR THIS NEXT-LEVEL SALAD.

INGREDIENTS

- ½ cup warm Jasmine Rice (page 131)
- 2 cups mesclun greens
- 1 cup chopped romaine lettuce
- 1 cup gently torn Boston lettuce
- ¼ cup thinly sliced red bell pepper
- ¼ cup thinly sliced green bell pepper
- ¼ cup shredded carrots
- ¼ cup Crispy Fried Shallots (page 129)
- 2 tablespoons torn Thai basil leaves
- ½ cup Spicy Basil Eggplant (page 125)
- ⅓ cup Thai Chili and Miso Dressing (page 141)

DIRECTIONS

Combine all of the ingredients in a large stainless-steel bowl. Top with the dressing and, using tongs, toss until well mixed and dressed.

Togarashi Steak Salad

◦ SERVES 1 ◦

The Tuna Provençale Salad (page 54) that we offer only in the summer was an instant hit, so we were inspired to build on its flavor profile to create this autumn/winter steak salad. The steak comes on a bed of soba noodles, shredded bok choy, assorted greens, and edamame, drizzled with a creamy Japanese sesame dressing and speckled with black and white sesame seeds. If you haven't already tried Kewpie mayonnaise (a Japanese mainstay), you're in for a treat here, as it is the base of our Kewpie Dressing (page 146).

INGREDIENTS

- ½ cup cooked soba noodles
- 3 cups shredded curly kale
- 1 cup thinly sliced bok choy
- ½ avocado, diced
- ¼ cup frozen edamame, thawed and rinsed
- ¼ cup shredded carrots
- ¼ cup shredded red cabbage
- ¼ cup diced cucumber
- ¼ cup sliced scallions
- 2 tablespoons sesame seeds (black and white)
- 2 tablespoons minced nori
- 4 ounces Seared Filet Mignon (page 120), sliced

- ⅓ cup Kewpie Dressing (page 146)

DIRECTIONS

Combine all of the ingredients except for the Seared Filet Mignon in a large stainless-steel bowl. Top with the dressing and, using tongs, toss until well mixed and dressed. Transfer to a serving bowl and arrange the filet mignon slices over top.

Smoked Meat Salad

◦ SERVES 1 ◦

This salad is an ode to Montreal, pure and simple. If you're from here or you've visited our city, you're sure to have had a salty, juicy warm smoked meat sandwich with bright vinegary yellow mustard on fresh rye bread with a side of pickles, chips, or fries at Schwartz's, Lester's Deli, Smoke Meat Pete, or Snowdon Deli. In our version of this salad, we use Lester Deli's smoked meat. This salad goes on our menu every November.

INGREDIENTS

- 4 cups chopped romaine lettuce
- Big handful Cape Cod kettle chips
- ¼ cup diced dill pickle (about 1 small pickle)
- 4 ounces sliced Montreal smoked meat, warmed and shredded
- ⅓ cup Baseball Mustard Dressing (page 150)

DIRECTIONS

Combine all of the ingredients except for the smoked meat in a large stainless-steel bowl. Top with the dressing and, using tongs, toss until well mixed and dressed.

Transfer to a serving bowl and add the smoked meat over top.

Christmas Stuffing Salad

∘ SERVES 4 ∘

After one holiday dinner, stuffed to the gills, we asked ourselves if we could make a salad for the family that revolved around the awesomeness of stuffing—obviously the best part of any holiday meal—and the delicious and varied sides to the turkey.

NOTE: IF YOU'RE MAKING THIS SALAD FROM SCRATCH, YOU'LL NEED SOME TIME TO PREPARE THE DIFFERENT COMPONENTS, BUT IF YOU'VE ALREADY ENJOYED YOUR THANKSGIVING OR CHRISTMAS MEAL, IT'S THE PERFECT SALAD TO MAKE USE OF EXTRA CRANBERRY SAUCE, LEFTOVER ROASTED VEG, AND YOUR FAVORITE STUFFING!

INGREDIENTS

- 12 cups mesclun greens
- 4 cups arugula
- 2 cups Roasted Vegetable Medley (page 83)
- 2 cups Brie Stuffing (page 83)
- 2 cups Homemade Garlic and Rosemary Pita Chips (page 130)
- ½ cup dried cranberries

- 1⅓ cups Cranberry Dressing (page 143)

DIRECTIONS

Combine all of the ingredients in a large stainless-steel bowl. Top with the dressing and, using tongs, toss until well mixed and dressed.

ROASTED VEGETABLE MEDLEY

MAKES 2 CUPS

INGREDIENTS

- 2 cups diced eggplant
- 2 cups diced zucchini
- 2 cups diced red onion
- 1 tablespoon minced sage
- 1 tablespoon thyme leaves
- 1 tablespoon minced rosemary
- ¼ cup olive oil
- 2 teaspoons salt
- 1 teaspoon freshly ground black pepper

NOTE: YOU MAY CHOOSE ANY NUMBER AND VARIETY OF VEGETABLES TO ROAST; JUST CUT THEM ALL INTO ½-INCH CUBES.

DIRECTIONS

Preheat the oven to 425°F.

In a large bowl, toss the eggplant, zucchini, onion, sage, thyme, and rosemary with the olive oil, salt, and pepper.

Spread the vegetables onto a parchment-lined sheet tray. Roast for 35 to 40 minutes until soft and browned. Remove from the oven, set aside to cool, and then transfer to an airtight container and refrigerate until ready to use. They will keep for up to 5 days.

BRIE STUFFING

MAKES 3 CUPS

YOU WILL NEED

- 8-inch square baking dish

INGREDIENTS

- ¼ cup unsalted butter
- ½ cup diced onion
- 1 cup diced Granny Smith apple
- ⅓ cup pecan halves, coarsely chopped
- 1 teaspoon minced rosemary
- 1 teaspoon minced sage
- 1 teaspoon minced thyme
- ½ teaspoon salt
- ½ teaspoon freshly ground black pepper
- 2 cups cubed (1-inch cubes) fresh sourdough bread or baguette
- 1 egg, beaten
- ¼ cup minced flat-leaf parsley
- ¼ to ½ cup chicken broth
- 2 ounces Brie cheese, cut into ½-inch cubes (about ½ cup)

DIRECTIONS

Preheat the oven to 425°F.

Grease and line an 8-inch square baking dish with parchment paper, leaving some overhang (for lifting out the stuffing later).

Melt the butter in a large frying pan over medium heat. Add the onion, apple, pecans, rosemary, sage, and thyme. Cook, stirring occasionally, until the onion and apple have softened and the mixture is fragrant, approximately 5 minutes. Stir in the salt and pepper.

Transfer the mixture to a large bowl. Add the cubes of bread, the beaten egg, the parsley, and enough broth so the dressing seems well moistened, stirring well. Add the cubes of Brie and stir some more.

Transfer the stuffing to the baking dish, patting it down well. Bake, uncovered, for 25 to 30 minutes or until the top is beginning to brown. Check to make sure the interior is still moist; if it's not, add a splash more broth and return to the oven for a further 5 to 10 minutes.

Remove from the oven and set aside to cool. Lift the stuffing out of the baking dish using the parchment handles, then cut or tear it into bite-size pieces. Transfer to an airtight container and refrigerate until ready to use. This will keep for up to 5 days.

Superfood 2.0 Salad

◦ SERVES 1 ◦

Another January, another set of resolutions for eating right, getting fitter, having less screen time, more outdoor time, more adventure . . . are we right?! This killer salad is a super fun January/New Year salad chock-full of different superfoods that support everyone's new-year, new-you resolutions. It's full of color, vibing with explosive flavors, and a fun way to incorporate some new elements (amaranth! moringa!) into your diet.

NOTE: AMARANTH IS A GLUTEN-FREE GRAIN (DATING BACK TO THE AZTECS) THAT IS HIGH IN PROTEIN AND LYSINE, AN ESSENTIAL AMINO ACID, AND REPLETE WITH FIBER AND IRON! THE MORINGA LEAF IN THE DRESSING FOR THIS RECIPE HAS BEEN USED IN INDIA IN TRADITIONAL HERBAL MEDICINE FOR CENTURIES. IT IS RICH IN ANTIOXIDANTS AND A SIGNIFICANT SOURCE OF VITAMINS AND PROTEIN.

INGREDIENTS

- ¼ cup Amaranth (page 131)
- 2 cups mesclun greens
- 2 cups baby spinach
- ½ cup Kimchi Brussels Sprouts (page 128)
- ¼ cup Pickled Super Veg (page 84)
- ¼ cup slivered almonds, toasted

- ⅓ cup Moringa Dressing (page 146)

DIRECTIONS

Combine all of the ingredients in a large stainless-steel bowl. Top with the dressing and, using tongs, toss until well mixed and dressed.

Shish Taouk-Inspired Salad

◦ SERVES 1 ◦

MANDY | Montreal is such a great place to be for authentic, delicious Middle Eastern food, and Lebanese food in particular. We are so lucky here to have so many fabulous restaurants to choose from. I'm also lucky to have a Lebanese husband, Mike, who can attest to their authenticity! As a family, we have enjoyed so many meals at the wonderful Daou, La Sirène de la Mer, and Garage Beirut, to name just a few faves. Oh, and for upscale Middle Eastern with a killer wine list, we highly recommend Restaurant Damas.

This vegetarian salad is a riff on the classic flavors we associate with shish taouk (marinated grilled chicken) and includes other delectable ingredients we associate with Levantine cuisine: pine nuts, pomegranate seeds, bulgur wheat (cracked whole-grain kernels of wheat), and generous amounts of fresh mint and parsley.

INGREDIENTS

- ½ cup Bulgur Wheat (page 131)
- 2 cups mesclun greens
- 2 cups chopped iceberg lettuce
- ¼ cup diced cucumber
- ¼ cup canned chickpeas, drained and rinsed
- ¼ cup halved cherry tomatoes
- ¼ cup Quick-Pickled Red Onion (page 123)
- 2 tablespoons pomegranate seeds
- 2 tablespoons toasted pine nuts
- 2 tablespoons torn mint leaves
- 2 tablespoons flat-leaf parsley leaves

- ⅓ cup Levantine Dressing (page 147)

DIRECTIONS

Combine all of the ingredients in a large stainless-steel bowl. Top with the dressing and, using tongs, toss until well mixed and dressed.

Dude Ranch Salad

◦ SERVES 1 ◦

Every February, we try to honor the spirit of the month in one of two ways: with a Valentine's Day lovey/heart-health awareness salad OR with a decadent throw-caution-and-health-to-the-wind Superbowl kind of salad. This salad might be one of the second type! Dorito-coated popcorn chicken bites with a ranch dressing? Pass the jalapeño poppers and the remote. Note to Doritos fans: we taste-tested "Cool Ranch" flavor versus "Nacho Cheese" flavor for the popcorn chicken recipe and were as surprised as you are that nacho cheese was a far superior coating for the chicken. The ranch was simply too overpowering and tangy and just didn't work. But pound for pound, they're still the best flavor of Doritos, if you ask us.

INGREDIENTS

- 3 cups chopped romaine lettuce
- 1 cup chopped iceberg lettuce
- ¼ cup halved cherry tomatoes
- ¼ cup thinly sliced celery
- ¼ cup grated strong white cheddar
- 2 tablespoons cilantro leaves
- 2 tablespoons sliced scallions
- ½ cup Dorito Popcorn Chicken (page 118)

- ⅓ cup Ranch Dressing (page 137)

DIRECTIONS

Combine all of the ingredients except for the Dorito Popcorn Chicken in a large stainless-steel bowl. Top with the dressing and, using tongs, toss until well mixed and dressed.

Transfer to a serving bowl and arrange the Dorito Popcorn Chicken over top.

Love Salad

◦ SERVES 1 ◦

This winter salad just wants to brighten everyone's mood and taste buds: it's Valentine-inspired red, pink, and delicious! It combines berries (much needed at this time of year), beets, and spicy roasted nuts with a sprinkling of creamy goat cheese. To stay in the full spirit of the season, you can substitute pomegranate seeds for the strawberries or blueberries, and of course you can make this salad year round.

NOTE: YOU CAN FIND COOKED BEETS IN SOUS-VIDE PACKAGING AT YOUR LOCAL GROCER, TYPICALLY IN THE REFRIGERATED AISLE.

INGREDIENTS

- ½ cup Quinoa (page 132)
- 4 cups mesclun greens
- ¼ cup sliced strawberries
- ¼ cup fresh blueberries
- ¼ cup diced cooked beets
- ¼ cup crumbled goat cheese
- ¼ cup Spicy Rosemary Nuts (page 130)

- ⅓ cup Very Berry Dressing (page 148)

DIRECTIONS

Combine all of the ingredients in a large stainless-steel bowl. Top with the dressing and, using tongs, toss until well mixed and dressed.

Grapefruit Salad

◦ SERVES 1 ◦

REBECCA | Many years ago, my good friend Joanna Fox (now a food writer!) gave Mandy a recipe for a hoisin-glazed salmon that came with the tastiest and tangiest yogurt sauce of all time. Mandy started making it, and making it, and . . . dipping her veggies in it, putting it in sandwiches, treating it as a condiment . . . until one day it just had to become a salad dressing. Its lime, ginger, and mint elements really complement the elements of this super fresh salad.

NOTE: HOW TO CUT A GRAPEFRUIT INTO SEGMENTS: PLACE THE WHOLE GRAPEFRUIT ON A CHOPPING BOARD AND, USING A SHARP PARING KNIFE, CUT AWAY THE PEEL AND THE PITH OF THE FRUIT, WORKING IN SECTIONS, UNTIL THE FLESH IS COMPLETELY EXPOSED. HOLDING THE FRUIT OVER A SMALL BOWL (TO COLLECT THE JUICES), USE THE KNIFE TO SLICE BETWEEN EACH MEMBRANE TO RELEASE THE INDIVIDUAL SEGMENTS. SET ASIDE.

YOU CAN FIND COOKED BEETS IN SOUS-VIDE PACKAGING AT YOUR LOCAL GROCER, TYPICALLY IN THE REFRIGERATED AISLE.

INGREDIENTS

- 3 cups mesclun greens
- 1 cup baby spinach leaves
- ½ avocado, diced
- ¼ cup shredded carrots
- ¼ cup shredded red cabbage
- ¼ cup very thinly sliced fennel
- ¼ cup diced cucumber
- ¼ cup diced cooked beets
- ¼ cup diced pear
- ½ cup segmented grapefruit (see note)
- 2 tablespoons Quick-Pickled Red Onion (page 123)
- 2 tablespoons pecan halves, toasted
- 2 tablespoons torn mint leaves

- ⅓ cup Creamy Ginger Mint Dressing (page 147)

DIRECTIONS

Combine all of the ingredients in a large stainless-steel bowl. Top with the dressing and, using tongs, toss until well mixed and dressed.

Island Chicken Salad

∘ SERVES 4 ∘

Before we helped found the Welcome Collective in 2017, we partnered with other Montreal charities, and one of our favorites is the Kanpe Foundation, co-founded by Régine Chassagne, of Arcade Fire fame, and Dominique Anglade, now the leader of the Quebec Liberal Party. "Kanpe" means "to stand up" in Haitian Creole. The foundation's mission is to support local organizations in their work with the most vulnerable communities in Haiti. A long history of Haitian immigration to Quebec has given Montreal the benefit of a rich cultural, social, and gastronomic Haitian influence—and inspired this salad, which appears every February on our menu.

NOTE: THE COMPONENTS FOR THIS SALAD REQUIRE A LITTLE ADVANCE PREP WORK AND SOME MARINATING, BUT IT'S A PERFECT PROJECT FOR A GENEROUS WEEKEND DINNER—AND WHY WE RECOMMEND YOU SERVE IT UP FAMILY-STYLE!

INGREDIENTS

∘ 8 to 10 cups mesclun greens
∘ 4 cups stemmed watercress
∘ 1 recipe Island Rice and Beans (page 96)
∘ ½ cup pickled jalapeño pepper rings
∘ 1 cup mandarin orange segments
∘ 1 recipe Island Chicken (page 96)

∘ 1⅓ cups Épis-Style Dressing (page 149)

DIRECTIONS

On a large platter, arrange a bed of the mesclun greens and watercress. Top with the rice and beans, pickled jalapeño, and orange segments. Drizzle with the dressing, and top with the chicken.

ISLAND CHICKEN

MAKES 8 PIECES

INGREDIENTS

- ¼ cup lime juice
- ¼ cup orange juice
- 1 tablespoon brown sugar
- 2 tablespoons olive oil
- 1 Scotch bonnet chili pepper, seeded and coarsely chopped (use gloves!)
- 2 tablespoons sliced scallions
- 2 cloves garlic, minced
- 1 tablespoon rosemary leaves
- 1 teaspoon ground allspice
- 1 teaspoon salt
- 1 teaspoon freshly ground black pepper
- 4 whole bone-in, skin-on chicken legs (separated into 4 thighs and 4 drumsticks)

DIRECTIONS

In a blender, combine all of the ingredients except for the chicken. Process on medium-high speed until smooth and well combined, 15 to 20 seconds.

Place the chicken thighs and drumsticks in a bowl or container and pour the marinade over top. Cover and refrigerate for a minimum of 2 hours (or overnight).

Preheat the oven to 425°F.

Spread the chicken pieces out on a parchment-lined sheet tray, discarding any excess marinade, and roast for 35 minutes, or until the chicken is cooked through. Remove from the oven and keep warm until ready to serve.

ISLAND RICE AND BEANS

MAKES 6 CUPS

YOU WILL NEED

- 8-inch square baking dish

INGREDIENTS

- 2 tablespoons olive oil
- ½ cup finely chopped onion
- 2 sliced scallions
- 3 cloves garlic, minced
- 1 tablespoon thyme leaves
- 1 tablespoon ground allspice
- 1 teaspoon brown sugar
- 1 teaspoon salt
- 1 teaspoon freshly ground black pepper
- 1½ cups long-grain rice
- 1½ cups canned black beans, drained and rinsed
- 1¾ cups coconut milk
- 2 cups low-sodium chicken broth

It is hard to make a very small batch of rice and beans, but this recipe is so tasty you won't regret having leftovers. It's our trusty recipe tester Kendra McKnight's favorite recipe in the book!

DIRECTIONS

Preheat the oven to 350°F.

In a sauté pan set over medium heat, add the olive oil and gently sauté the onion, scallions, and garlic until translucent. Stir in the thyme, allspice, sugar, salt, and pepper, and continue to cook for another minute or so, until fragrant. Add the rice to the pan, stirring to coat.

Transfer the contents of the pan to an 8-inch square baking dish, and gently but thoroughly stir in the beans, coconut milk, and chicken broth until all of the ingredients look evenly distributed in the liquid.

Bake for 45 minutes until the rice looks soft and puffed but still tastes a little firm. Set aside in a warm place until ready to serve.

Jerk-Spiced Shrimp Salad

∘ SERVES 1 ∘

Here we have created a spicy tropical salad with fresh seafood to marry some of our favorite Caribbean flavors—in this case, Matane shrimp (in season in the St. Lawrence River from March to April) seasoned with Jamaican jerk spices and paired with pikliz, an irresistible pickle/condiment staple in the Haitian pantry.

It's a very Montreal dish, which is to say: come spring, we are desperate for a hit of tanginess and a burst of bold flavors avec maritime seafood, but we still have to eat it wearing our snow-covered Sorels. Summer is coming, but there is at least one more blizzard in store.

NOTE: THIS RECIPE TAKES SOME PREP TIME—IT'S BEST TO MAKE THE PIKLIZ A DAY OR TWO AHEAD OF TIME, GIVING IT THE OCCASIONAL STIR UNTIL READY TO USE—BUT IT'S WELL WORTH IT.

INGREDIENTS

- 2 cups chopped romaine lettuce
- 1 cup mesclun greens
- 1 cup arugula
- ¼ cup diced mango
- ¼ cup Pikliz (page 123)
- ¼ cup plantain chips
- 2 tablespoons coarsely chopped toasted cashews
- ½ cup Jerk-Spiced Shrimp (see below)

- ⅓ cup Tropical Avocado Dressing (page 138)

DIRECTIONS

Combine all of the ingredients except for the Jerk-Spiced Shrimp in a large stainless-steel bowl. Top with the dressing and, using tongs, toss until well mixed and dressed. Transfer to a serving bowl and arrange the shrimp over top.

JERK-SPICED SHRIMP

MAKES 2 CUPS

INGREDIENTS

- 3 cups Matane shrimp, thawed and patted dry
- 1½ tablespoons Jerk-Style Seasoning (page 133)
- 2 tablespoons olive oil

DIRECTIONS

Preheat the oven to 350°F.

Combine the shrimp, Jerk-Style Seasoning, and olive oil in a bowl. Mix with your hands until the shrimp are evenly coated.

Transfer the shrimp to a parchment-lined sheet tray and bake for 8 minutes, or until the shrimp are fully cooked. Remove from the oven, set aside to cool, and then transfer to an airtight container and refrigerate until ready to use. They will keep for up to 3 days.

Citrus and Steak Salad

∘ SERVES 1 ∘

MANDY | Inspired by my travels through Southeast Asia, this salad is a mix of all things fresh and citrusy, with the unmistakably satisfying crunch of fried wonton strips and a zesty ginger lime dressing. This salad is always a hit when we add it to our monthly salad menu, usually in September or October. We love adding some steak to it (page 120). The lime punch of the salad gives it a light twist, to create the perfect cold steak and noodle salad.

INGREDIENTS

- 1 cup Rice Noodles (page 132)
- 3 cups mesclun greens
- ¼ cup frozen edamame, thawed and rinsed
- ¼ cup diced red bell pepper
- ½ avocado, diced
- ¼ cup sliced scallions
- ¼ cup sliced wonton wrappers, fried
- ½ cup Spicy Pineapple Crunch (page 129)
- 2 tablespoons cilantro leaves
- 4 ounces Seared Filet Mignon (page 120), sliced (optional)

- ⅓ cup Ginger Lime Dressing (page 139)

DIRECTIONS

Combine all of the ingredients in a large stainless-steel bowl. Top with the dressing and, using tongs, toss until well mixed and dressed.

Cabane à Sucre

Heading to the "cabane à sucre" (sugar shack) in March and April, once the snow starts to melt and the maple tree sap starts to flow, is a beloved yearly ritual here in Quebec. (Fun fact: Quebec produces 75 percent of the world's supply of maple syrup.)

At the sugar shack, you share long picnic tables with other groups of families and friends, and you have the brunch of your life: fried eggs, pancakes, pork rinds, smoked ham, bacon, sausage, cretons (pork spread), and every other possible remaining pork product, and ALL OF IT is generously drenched in maple syrup. Then, after a horse-drawn sleigh ride through the maple forest, you get to enjoy "tire à l'érable" outside: hot maple taffy is poured over fresh snow, and you wrap the thick, hardening syrup around a popsicle stick. It's out of this world, and even after your feast, you somehow find room for a few of those.

Every family has a favorite sugar shack, and we love these in particular:

Au Pied de Cochon
La P'tite Cabane d'la Côte
Érablière Jean Parent

La Tablée des Pionniers in
Saint-Faustin-Lac-Carré
(where we used to go as kids)

Cabane à Sucre Salad

Here's our salad take on the whole "cabane à sucre" (sugar shack) experience, and it includes our house dressing, which also contains maple syrup!

INGREDIENTS

- 2 cups shredded curly kale
- 2 cups chopped romaine lettuce
- ¼ cup diced apples
- ¼ cup shredded carrots
- ¼ cup diced maple-smoked ham
- ¼ cup diced cooked bacon
- ¼ cup dried cranberries
- ¼ cup kettle chips (we like the Cape Cod ones)
- ¼ cup sliced scallions
- ¼ cup Candied Pecans (page 128)

- ⅓ cup Spicy Maple Dressing (page 148)

DIRECTIONS

Combine all of the ingredients a large stainless-steel bowl. Top with the dressing and, using tongs, toss until well mixed and dressed.

Spicy Meat Salad

∘ SERVES 1 ∘

In the Venn diagram of cravings, this salad sits right where Delta Phi frat boy and second-trimester pregnant lady overlap—and all three of the authors of this book happen to know a lot about those kinds of cravings. Not to worry if you don't fit into one of those categories; the truth is, everyone loves this salad. It is a bit of an everything-but-the-kitchen-sink salad, from the hot peppers to the chips to the cheddar—so feel free to improvise to get your own cravings into the mix by adding or substituting veggies like cherry tomatoes or shredded cabbage. Also, this would be the salad to favor high-quality artisan-crafted cured meats. In Montreal, you can't beat Phillip Viens's mortadella!

INGREDIENTS

- 2 cups chopped romaine lettuce
- 2 cups chopped iceberg lettuce
- ½ avocado, diced
- ½ cup chopped sliced mortadella
- ½ cup cubed Genoa salami
- ¼ cup shredded mature cheddar
- ¼ cup Crispy Fried Shallots (page 129)
- Big handful Ruffles Sour Cream & Onion chips
- 2 tablespoons pickled banana pepper rings

- ⅓ cup Spicy Sriracha Dressing (page 150)

DIRECTIONS

Combine all of the ingredients in a large stainless-steel bowl. Top with the dressing and, using tongs, toss until well mixed and dressed.

Casablanca Salad

◦ SERVES 1 ◦

We love spices. When we learn about one that is new to us, we tend to go through a deep exploratory phase, and often a special salad comes out of it. In this case, the star of the show is ras el hanout, a staple of the Moroccan kitchen. The name of this blend translates to "head of the shop" or "top shelf," and it includes ground ginger, cardamom, cinnamon, coriander, nutmeg, allspice, cloves, and various peppers. The blend is so versatile, we've used it to make a vegan crumble. The salad does include feta, but if you want a completely plant-based salad, just omit the cheese.

INGREDIENTS

- ½ cup Pearl Couscous (page 132)
- 4 cups mesclun greens
- ¼ cup halved red grapes
- ¼ cup diced dried apricots
- ½ cup Ras el Hanout Vegan Crumble (page 119)
- ¼ cup crumbled feta
- 2 tablespoons coarsely chopped toasted pistachios
- 2 tablespoons torn mint leaves
- 2 tablespoons coarsely chopped flat-leaf parsley

- ⅓ cup Lemon Cinnamon Dressing (page 151)

DIRECTIONS

Combine all of the ingredients in a large stainless-steel bowl. Top with the dressing and, using tongs, toss until well mixed and dressed.

Miso Salad

◦ SERVES 1 ◦

MANDY | There was a time in 2014 when Becca and I were both pregnant with our second kids—Sonny and Charlie—and we were both craving crunchy, super colorful salads, and we were both obsessed with miso-flavored anything. I was also eating apples dipped in peanut butter as a snack all day long and wanting to make some kind of salad out of that . . . and the combination of all those things is how I got to this Miso Salad. We were both working out of our Westmount location, bumping bellies and asking each other every day if we were in the mood for "our" salad. We would also suggest it to every customer who came in asking how we were feeling and what we were eating in those big-bellied days. All baby bump memories aside, though, this is a straight-up delicious salad whatever state you're in, any time of year.

INGREDIENTS

- 3 cups chopped romaine lettuce
- 1 cup mesclun greens
- ½ cup Mock Chicken (page 117)
- ½ avocado, diced
- ¼ cup frozen edamame, thawed and rinsed
- ¼ cup diced red bell pepper
- ¼ cup shredded carrot
- ¼ cup sliced scallions
- ¼ cup diced Granny Smith apple
- 1 tablespoon unsalted peanuts, toasted and coarsely chopped

- ⅓ cup Miso Ginger Dressing (page 151)

DIRECTIONS

Combine all of the ingredients in a large stainless-steel bowl. Top with the dressing and, using tongs, toss until well mixed and dressed.

Spicy Kani Salad

◦ SERVES 1 ◦

Kani surimi is a paste made from white fish (primarily pollock), soy, egg white, and starch that's then shaped to look like the leg meat of snow crab or Japanese spider crab. This salad celebrates kani as a delicacy in its own right! And it is a sensational salad: the pops of green from the delicate bok choy and the edamame, the deep salty forest green of shredded nori, the crispiness of the fried shallots, the creamy avocado, the perfectly dressed crabmeat, and the satiating rice make this a delectable, hearty meal. Of course, if imitation crabmeat isn't your thing, you can use real crab when it's in season.

INGREDIENTS

- ½ cup Jasmine Rice (page 131)
- 2 cups chopped romaine lettuce
- 1 cup mesclun greens
- 1 cup thinly sliced bok choy
- ½ avocado, diced
- ¼ cup frozen edamame, thawed and rinsed
- ¼ cup Crispy Fried Shallots (page 129)
- 2 tablespoons minced nori
- 2 tablespoons sesame seeds
- ½ cup Spicy Kani (see below)

- ⅓ cup Smooth Sesame Dressing (page 136)

DIRECTIONS

Combine all of the ingredients except for the Spicy Kani in a large stainless-steel bowl. Top with the dressing and, using tongs, toss until well mixed and dressed.

Transfer to a serving bowl and arrange the Spicy Kani over top.

SPICY KANI

MAKES 2 CUPS

INGREDIENTS

- 1 pound kani (imitation crabmeat)
- ⅓ cup mayonnaise
- 2 teaspoons Sriracha sauce
- 2 cloves garlic, minced
- Zest and juice of 1 lemon

DIRECTIONS

Place the crab sticks in a bowl and use your hands to break the flesh into nice flaked bite-size pieces. Stir in the mayonnaise, Sriracha, garlic, and lemon zest and juice until the crabmeat is evenly coated. Transfer to an airtight container and refrigerate until ready to use. The Spicy Kani will keep for up to 3 days.

Teriyaki Tofu Salad

◦ SERVES 1 ◦

We've been proudly preparing and serving teriyaki tofu at Mandy's for many years, and the recipe has not changed. We wanted to achieve that sticky-sweet-spicy taste of ribs from our favorite Montreal Chinese restaurants like Peking Garden and Aunt Dai, but using versatile and vegan tofu. This whole salad is vegan (you can swap in maple or agave syrup for the honey if you're strictly vegan) and filling in the healthiest sense of the word.

NOTE: RAW CELERIAC TENDS TO OXIDIZE VERY QUICKLY—AS SOON AS YOU CUT INTO IT. TO KEEP IT CRUNCHY AND LOOKING FRESHLY CUT, TRANSFER THE CUT CELERIAC TO AN AIRTIGHT CONTAINER AND COVER WITH COLD WATER. COVER AND REFRIGERATE UNTIL READY TO USE, SIMPLY PATTING IT DRY BEFORE ADDING IT TO YOUR SALAD.

INGREDIENTS

- 2 cups shredded curly kale
- 2 cups mesclun greens
- ½ cup Teriyaki Tofu (page 120)
- ½ avocado, diced
- ¼ cup shredded carrot
- ¼ cup julienned celeriac (see note)
- ¼ cup small broccoli florets
- ¼ cup sliced scallions
- 2 tablespoons coarsely chopped cashews
- 2 tablespoons sesame seeds
- 2 tablespoons cilantro leaves

- ⅓ cup Sweet Tamari Dressing (page 136)

DIRECTIONS

Combine all of the ingredients in a large stainless-steel bowl. Top with the dressing and, using tongs, toss until well mixed and dressed.

SALAD ADDITIONS

The following recipes can be added to almost any of the salads in the book for a bit more substance or crunch.

Proteins

ROASTED CHICKEN BREAST

MAKES 1½ CUPS
(4 TO 6 PORTIONS)

INGREDIENTS

- 1 large (10-ounce) skinless boneless chicken breast
- 1 tablespoon olive oil
- 1 teaspoon Montreal steak spice (see note on page 195)

DIRECTIONS

Preheat the oven to 375°F.

Rub the chicken breast with the olive oil and steak spice.

Place on a small parchment-lined sheet tray and roast until the internal temperature registers 165°F on an instant-read digital thermometer, 25 to 30 minutes.

Remove from the oven and set aside to cool. Then cut into ½-inch cubes. The cubed chicken will keep, refrigerated, in an airtight container for up to 5 days.

MOCK CHICKEN

MAKES 2 CUPS
(4 PORTIONS)

INGREDIENTS

- 1 14-ounce (400 g) package firm tofu, unopened
- 2 tablespoons tamari
- 2 tablespoons nutritional yeast flakes
- 1 teaspoon salt
- ½ teaspoon freshly ground black pepper
- 2 tablespoons avocado oil

DIRECTIONS

Place the unopened package of tofu in the freezer for 24 hours or longer.

Defrost the tofu at room temperature until soft and squishy, about 3 hours. This helps the tofu keep its form.

Open the package and drain the tofu over the sink, squeezing and pressing with your hands to remove excess liquid. Then, working over a large bowl, use your hands to crumble the tofu into small bite-size pieces (no bigger than 1 inch each).

Toss the crumbled tofu with the tamari, nutritional yeast, salt, and pepper.

In a large frying pan over medium heat, warm the avocado oil. Add the tofu and cook until golden brown, stirring regularly, about 5 minutes.

Remove from the heat and allow to cool. The mock chicken will keep, refrigerated, in an airtight container for up to 7 days.

SATAY MOCK CHICKEN

**MAKES 2 CUPS
(4 PORTIONS)**

INGREDIENTS

- 1 cup roasted peanuts
- 3 tablespoons brown sugar
- 2 cloves garlic, minced
- ½ teaspoon red pepper flakes
- ⅓ cup coconut milk
- ¼ cup tamari
- 1 teaspoon lime juice
- ¼ cup hot water
- Salt and freshly ground black pepper
- 2 cups Mock Chicken (page 117) or 4 portions of cooked protein of your choice

For that Satay Mock Chicken Salad (page 50) or enjoyable on its own! The satay marinade is super versatile and can be used with any cooked protein of your choice.

DIRECTIONS

In a blender, combine the peanuts, sugar, garlic, red pepper flakes, coconut milk, tamari, and lime juice. Process on medium-high speed until smooth and well combined, 15 to 20 seconds. Stop the blender and scrape down the sides of the jar with a spatula as needed.

With the blender running on low speed, slowly drizzle in the hot water until the marinade is emulsified and thickened, about 30 seconds. Season to taste with salt and pepper. Transfer to an airtight container and refrigerate until ready to use.

In a medium bowl, coat the Mock Chicken with 1 cup of the marinade and refrigerate for 6 hours or overnight. Extra marinade will keep refrigerated in an airtight container for up to 7 days.

Preheat the oven to 350°F.

Spread the marinated Mock Chicken out on a parchment-lined sheet tray, discarding any excess marinade. Bake for 10 minutes until golden.

Remove from the oven and set aside to cool at room temperature. Transfer to an airtight container and refrigerate until ready to use. The Satay Mock Chicken will keep, refrigerated, for up to 7 days.

DORITO POPCORN CHICKEN

**MAKES 2 CUPS
(4 PORTIONS)**

INGREDIENTS

- 1 9-ounce (255 g) bag Nacho Cheese Doritos tortilla chips
- 1 large (10-ounce) skinless boneless chicken breast, cut into ½-inch cubes
- 1 tablespoon olive or avocado oil
- 2 teaspoons Tabasco hot sauce
- ¼ teaspoon salt
- ¼ teaspoon freshly ground black pepper

DIRECTIONS

Preheat the oven to 425°F.

Transfer the Doritos into a large ziplock bag. Seal the bag, removing as much air out of it as you can. Use a rolling pin to crush the chips to a fine powder (similar results can be achieved with a few pulses in a food processor).

In a bowl, combine the cubed chicken with the oil, Tabasco, salt, and pepper and stir well to coat.

Place the chicken in the bag of Dorito crumbs, seal the bag, and start shaking! Make sure the chicken pieces are completely coated before transferring them to a sheet tray lined with parchment paper.

Bake for 15 minutes, or until crispy and cooked through. Remove from the oven and set aside to cool. Transfer to an airtight container and refrigerate until ready to use. This keeps for up to 3 days.

RAS EL HANOUT VEGAN CRUMBLE

MAKES 2 CUPS

INGREDIENTS

- 2½ cups Yves Veggie Ground Round
- 2 tablespoons ras el hanout spice blend
- 2 tablespoons lemon juice
- 1 tablespoon olive oil
- 1 tablespoon minced flat-leaf parsley
- 1 tablespoon minced mint
- ¼ teaspoon salt

NOTE: IF YOU CAN'T FIND YVES VEGGIE GROUND ROUND, A SOY-BASED SUBSTITUTE FOR GROUND BEEF, LOOK FOR OTHER VEGAN GROUND MEAT SUBSTITUTES AT YOUR LOCAL HEALTH FOOD STORE.

DIRECTIONS

Preheat the oven to 400°F.

In a large bowl, break up the ground round with your hands until it is fully crumbled, then mix in the ras el hanout, lemon juice, olive oil, minced herbs, and salt.

Spread the mixture evenly onto a parchment-lined sheet tray and bake for 5 minutes until fragrant.

Remove from the oven and set aside to cool. If not using immediately, transfer to an airtight container and refrigerate until ready to use. This will keep for up to 5 days.

ROASTED MARINATED TOFU

MAKES 2 CUPS
(4 PORTIONS)

INGREDIENTS

- 3 tablespoons avocado oil
- 2 tablespoons white miso
- 2 tablespoons tamari
- 2 tablespoons rice wine vinegar
- 2 tablespoons lime juice
- 2 tablespoons maple syrup
- 1 tablespoon lemon juice
- 1 tablespoon minced garlic
- 1 tablespoon minced ginger
- 2 teaspoons Sriracha sauce
- 2 teaspoons sambal oelek
- 1 14-ounce (400 g) block firm tofu, cut into ½-inch cubes

Tofu's taste neutrality often works against it—on its own it is not exactly the gold-medal winner in the flavor category. But the flip side is that it's a terrific sponge for absorbing other flavors. We douse ours in a trifecta of sweet, salty, and citrus for the best of all worlds.

NOTE: THE TOFU SHOULD BE MARINATED OVERNIGHT OR LONGER. PLAN ACCORDINGLY.

DIRECTIONS

In a bowl, combine the avocado oil, miso, tamari, vinegar, lime juice, maple syrup, lemon juice, garlic, ginger, Sriracha, and sambal oelek. Whisk until well blended.

Place the tofu cubes in a large ziplock bag and pour the marinade into the bag. Seal well, removing as much air from the bag as possible and making sure all the cubes are coated. Refrigerate overnight or up to 24 hours.

Preheat the oven to 425°F.

Spread the cubes, discarding any leftover marinade, on a large unlined sheet tray and roast for 5 minutes. Remove the tray from the oven, turn over the cubes of tofu, and roast for another 5 minutes. Turn the cubes one more time, and roast for a final 3 minutes or until all the tofu is golden brown and crispy. Remove from the oven and allow the tofu to cool completely, then refrigerate in an airtight container until ready to use. The cubed tofu will keep for up to 5 days.

TERIYAKI TOFU

MAKES 2 CUPS
(4 PORTIONS)

INGREDIENTS

- 1 tablespoon minced ginger
- 1 tablespoon minced garlic
- ½ cup tamari
- ¼ cup honey
- ⅓ cup lightly packed brown sugar
- 2 tablespoons sesame oil
- 2 tablespoons rice vinegar
- 1 teaspoon red pepper flakes
- 1 tablespoon cornstarch
- 1 16-ounce (454 g) block firm tofu, cut into ½-inch cubes

Sweet, salty, sticky, and spicy, this sauce is everything. While we opted to use it on tofu, it's equally good on just about any type of meat. Throw it on the barbecue, and it's even more divine. Works especially well with Rainbow Salad (page 62).

DIRECTIONS

In a bowl, combine the ginger, garlic, tamari, honey, brown sugar, sesame oil, vinegar, red pepper flakes, and cornstarch and whisk until well blended. Place the tofu cubes in the marinade and stir to coat evenly. Refrigerate for at least 3 to 6 hours and up to overnight (a shorter marinating time is possible in a pinch, but the flavor of the marinade will penetrate the tofu deeper the longer you let it sit).

Preheat the oven to 425°F.

Spread the cubes (marinade included) on a large unlined sheet tray and roast for 10 minutes. Remove the tray from the oven, turn over the cubes of tofu, and roast for another 5 minutes until all the tofu is golden brown and the sauce has caramelized and turned sticky. Remove from the oven and allow the tofu to cool completely, then refrigerate in an airtight container until ready to use. The cubed tofu will keep for up to 5 days.

SEARED FILET MIGNON

MAKES 4 PORTIONS

INGREDIENTS

- 1¼ pounds beef tenderloin, cut into 3 1-inch-thick steaks
- Salt and freshly ground black pepper
- 3 tablespoons togarashi (only needed if making the Togarashi Steak Salad, page 74)
- 2 tablespoons unsalted butter
- 2 tablespoons olive oil

We love this steak addition with the Citrus and Steak Salad in particular (page 98). The citrusy punch of the salad gives it a lighter twist, to create the perfect cold steak and noodle salad.

DIRECTIONS

Season the meat generously with the salt and pepper (and the togarashi if using).

Warm the butter and olive oil in a large frying pan over medium-high heat until bubbling and shimmering. Sear the steaks for 2 minutes on one side, then flip and continue cooking for approximately 3 more minutes for rare (or until the internal temperature registers 120°F on an instant-read digital thermometer), 6 minutes for medium-rare (130°F), or 7 minutes for medium (140°F) doneness.

Set the meat aside to rest for 5 minutes before slicing. Store in an airtight container in the fridge for up to 5 days.

SEARED TUNA FILLET

MAKES ONE
4-OUNCE PORTION

INGREDIENTS

- 2 tablespoons herbes de Provence
- 1 tablespoon minced oregano
- 1 teaspoon salt
- 1 teaspoon freshly ground black pepper
- 4 ounces center-cut tuna loin ("saku cut") or olive-oil packed tuna
- 2 tablespoons + 1 teaspoon olive oil (or oil from the jar of tuna)

NOTE: YOU CAN FIND HERBES DE PROVENCE—A BLEND OF DRIED ROSEMARY, THYME, MARJORAM, OREGANO, AND SAVORY—AT ANY GOURMET RETAILER OR SPECIALTY SPICE SHOP. COOKING A BLOCK OF TUNA TO RARE REQUIRES CAREFUL TIMING—BE WARNED THAT IT'S VERY EASY TO OVERCOOK THIS EXPENSIVE, PRIZED CUT OF FISH. CONSIDER USING A TIMER WHEN SEARING.

DIRECTIONS

In a shallow bowl, combine the herbes de Provence, oregano, salt, and pepper.

Pat the tuna steaks dry with paper towel, then rub them with 1 teaspoon of the olive oil. Evenly coat the block of tuna with the herb mixture, rubbing the seasoning into the fillet with your hands as needed.

In a nonstick frying pan over high heat, warm the remaining 2 tablespoons of olive oil. When the oil is very hot and just starting to smoke, add the tuna. Cook for 30 seconds, then lower the heat to medium-high and continue to cook until a crust forms, about 90 seconds. Using tongs, flip the tuna over and cook for 90 seconds more. The fish will be cooked on the outside but rare on the inside. Remove from the pan and transfer to a cutting board to cool. To serve, cut the tuna into ¼-inch-thick slices.

Pickles and Veg

PICKLED SUPER VEG

MAKES 2 CUPS
(8 PORTIONS)

INGREDIENTS

- ¾ cup julienned watermelon radish
- ¾ cup shredded red cabbage
- ¾ cup julienned carrots
- ¼ cup basil leaves, cut into long, thin strips
- 1½ cups granulated sugar
- 1½ cups apple cider vinegar
- 1 teaspoon salt

DIRECTIONS

Combine the radish, cabbage, carrots, and basil in a large heatproof bowl. Set aside.

Combine the sugar, vinegar, and salt in a saucepan and bring to a boil, whisking to dissolve the sugar. Let it simmer for 2 to 3 minutes, then pour the hot pickling liquid over the vegetables in the bowl. Cover the bowl tightly with plastic wrap and let it sit for 30 minutes.

Transfer the vegetables to a Mason jar or sealable container of your choice, including enough of the pickling liquid to cover them completely. Let cool completely, then refrigerate until ready to use. The pickled vegetables will keep, refrigerated in a sealed Mason jar or an airtight container, for up to 7 days.

PIKLIZ

**MAKES 4 CUPS
(8 PORTIONS)**

INGREDIENTS

- 2 cups packed shredded red cabbage
- ½ cup packed shredded carrots
- ¾ cup sliced scallions
- ¾ cup thinly sliced jalapeños
- 8 whole cloves
- 1 teaspoon dried thyme
- 2½ cups white vinegar
- ¼ cup lime juice
- 1 teaspoon salt

This piquant slaw definitely packs a punch—and its mouth-puckering, multi-layered tang elevates any salad or meat, such as slow roasted ribs or braised beef. We love it with our Seared Filet Mignon (page 120), our Island Rice and Beans (page 96), or added to the Island Chicken Salad (page 95). It's also spectacular in a sandwich (but drained thoroughly so you don't make your bread soggy) with pulled pork, mortadella, avocado, and lettuce with a healthy schmear of mayonnaise. We have this on hand in the fridge from August until April. Always.

DIRECTIONS

Toss the cabbage, carrots, scallions, jalapeños, cloves, and thyme in a large bowl and then transfer to a 4-cup Mason jar or sealable container of your choice.

Using the same the bowl, combine the vinegar, lime juice, and salt, and whisk until the salt dissolves. Pour the pickling liquid into the jar, covering the vegetables completely. Let sit at room temperature for 1 hour, then remove the cloves before using. These will keep, refrigerated in a sealed Mason jar or an airtight container, for up to 10 days.

QUICK-PICKLED RED ONION

**MAKES 1 CUP
(MAKES 8 PORTIONS)**

INGREDIENTS

- ½ cup apple cider vinegar
- 1 tablespoon granulated sugar
- 1 teaspoon salt
- 1 red onion, very thinly sliced

DIRECTIONS

In a small bowl, combine the vinegar, sugar, salt, with 1 cup of water and whisk until the sugar and salt dissolve.

Place the onion slices in a Mason jar or sealable container of your choice. Pour the pickling liquid into the jar, covering the onion completely. Let sit at room temperature for 1 hour before using. This will keep, refrigerated in a sealed Mason jar or an airtight container, for up to 10 days.

BA-CORN

MAKES 2 CUPS

INGREDIENTS

- 1½ cups canned corn kernels, drained and rinsed
- ½ pound thickly sliced bacon, cut into ¼-inch cubes (about 3 cups)
- ¼ teaspoon salt
- 1 teaspoon freshly ground black pepper

NOTE: THIS RECIPE CAN EASILY BE DOUBLED, BUT MAKE SURE YOU COOK THE BACON/CORN MIXTURE IN TWO BATCHES RATHER THAN OVERCROWDING ONE SHEET TRAY.

DIRECTIONS

Preheat the oven to 400°F.

In a large mixing bowl, combine the corn and bacon and season with the salt and pepper.

Place on a parchment-lined sheet tray and roast for 20 minutes (stirring every 6 to 7 minutes) until the bacon is crispy and the corn a deep golden color. Remove from the oven and set aside to cool, then transfer to an airtight container. This will keep in the fridge for up to 5 days.

ROASTED FENNEL AND LEEK

MAKES 2 CUPS

INGREDIENTS

- 2 cups sliced fennel (¼-inch slices)
- 3 cups sliced leeks (½-inch slices)
- Zest and juice of 1 lemon
- ½ teaspoon salt
- ½ teaspoon freshly ground black pepper
- ¼ cup olive oil

DIRECTIONS

Preheat the oven to 400°F.

In a large bowl, combine the fennel, leeks, lemon zest and juice, salt, and pepper and stir well. Drizzle with the olive oil and stir again.

Transfer the vegetable mixture to a parchment-lined sheet tray and roast for 25 to 30 minutes, until the leek and fennel look golden but not burned. Remove from the oven and set aside to cool. Use immediately or transfer to an airtight container and refrigerate until ready to use. This keeps for up to 5 days.

FIVE-SPICE ROASTED SQUASH

MAKES 2½ TO 3 CUPS

INGREDIENTS

- ½ cup unsalted butter, melted
- 1 teaspoon five-spice powder
- 1 teaspoon ground cinnamon
- ½ teaspoon salt
- ¾ cup lightly packed brown sugar
- 1 small butternut squash (about 2 pounds), cut into 1-inch cubes

DIRECTIONS

Preheat the oven to 400°F.

In a large bowl, whisk the melted butter, five-spice powder, cinnamon, and salt until combined. Add the sugar and whisk until it starts to dissolve. Place the cubed squash in the bowl and stir to coat.

Transfer the squash to a parchment-lined sheet tray and drizzle any remaining butter mixture over top. Roast for 8 to 10 minutes until beginning to soften, then stir and continue to roast for another 5 minutes until golden, glazed, fragrant, and soft.

Remove from the oven and set aside to cool. If not using immediately, transfer to an airtight container and refrigerate until ready to use. This will keep for up to 5 days.

ROASTED SWEET POTATO

MAKES ABOUT 1½ CUPS (6 PORTIONS)

INGREDIENTS

- 1 large sweet potato (about 1 pound)
- 1 tablespoon olive oil

When we feel like we "need" a side of fries with a salad, we throw in some roasted diced sweet potatoes instead. We love them in the Wolfe Bowl (from our first book), in the Shish Taouk–Inspired Salad (page 87), and even in the Casablanca Salad (page 105).

DIRECTIONS

Preheat the oven to 425°F.

Slice the sweet potato in half lengthwise. Brush the cut sides with the olive oil, then place face down on a small sheet tray.

Bake for 35 to 40 minutes or until the flesh feels tender but not mushy when you insert a small, sharp knife into the potato.

Remove from the oven and set aside to cool. Peel off the skin and discard. Cut the sweet potato into ½-inch cubes. The cubes will keep, refrigerated, in an airtight container for up to 5 days.

SPICY BASIL EGGPLANT

MAKES 2 CUPS

INGREDIENTS

- 2 small Chinese or Japanese eggplant, halved lengthwise and cut into ½-inch cubes
- ⅓ cup avocado oil
- 1 small white onion, thinly sliced
- 5 cloves garlic, thinly sliced
- 5 Thai chilies, minced (or ½ teaspoon red pepper flakes)
- 3 tablespoons fish sauce
- 2 tablespoons tamari
- ⅓ cup lightly packed brown sugar
- ¼ cup lime juice
- ¾ cup Thai basil leaves

DIRECTIONS

Preheat the oven to 400°F.

In a bowl, toss together the eggplant and avocado oil.

Spread the eggplant onto a parchment-lined sheet tray. Roast until the eggplant starts to brown, about 15 minutes. Remove from the oven, stir in the onion, garlic, and chilies and cook for a further 7 to 8 minutes.

In the meantime, whisk the fish sauce, tamari, brown sugar, lime juice, and ⅓ cup of warm water to combine. Pour the sauce over the eggplant and stir. Roast for another 10 minutes until the sauce starts to caramelize and turns syrupy.

Remove from the oven, stir in the Thai basil, and set aside to cool. Drain off any excess liquid, transfer to an airtight container, and refrigerate until ready to use. This will keep for up to 5 days.

PARMESAN BRUSSELS SPROUTS

MAKES 2 CUPS

INGREDIENTS

- 1 pound Brussels sprouts, halved
- 2 tablespoons olive oil
- ¼ teaspoon salt
- ¼ teaspoon freshly ground black pepper
- ¾ cup grated Parmesan

DIRECTIONS

Preheat the oven to 425°F.

In a bowl, toss the sprouts with the olive oil, salt, and pepper.

Spread the sprouts onto a parchment-lined sheet tray. Roast for 8 minutes, then sprinkle the Parmesan over top and roast for a further 4 minutes. Remove from the oven, set aside to cool, and then transfer to an airtight container and refrigerate until ready to use. This will keep for up to 5 days.

FENNEL-ROASTED CARROTS

MAKES 1½ CUPS

INGREDIENTS

- 1 pound rainbow carrots, halved lengthwise and cut into 1-inch pieces
- 2 tablespoons olive oil
- ¾ teaspoon fennel seeds
- ½ teaspoon salt
- ¼ teaspoon freshly ground black pepper

DIRECTIONS

Preheat the oven to 400°F.

In a bowl, toss the carrots with the olive oil, fennel seeds, salt, and pepper.

Spread the carrots onto a parchment-lined sheet tray. Roast for 25 to 30 minutes until soft and golden. Remove from the oven, set aside to cool, then transfer to an airtight container and refrigerate until ready to use.

ROASTED JERK-SPICED CORN

MAKES 1½ CUPS

INGREDIENTS

- 1½ cups canned corn kernels, drained, rinsed, and patted dry, or kernels from 2 ears of fresh corn
- 1 tablespoon olive oil
- 1 tablespoon Jerk-Style Seasoning (page 133)

DIRECTIONS

Preheat the oven to 375°F.

In a bowl, combine the corn kernels, olive oil, and Jerk-Style Seasoning.

Spread the seasoned corn evenly onto a parchment-lined sheet tray. Roast for 15 minutes, until the corn starts to brown slightly. Remove from the oven and set aside to cool, then refrigerate in an airtight container until ready to use. This will keep in the fridge for up to 5 days.

KIMCHI BRUSSELS SPROUTS

MAKES 2 CUPS

INGREDIENTS

- 1½ cups store-bought napa cabbage kimchi
- 1 pound Brussels sprouts, trimmed and quartered
- 2 tablespoons olive oil
- ½ teaspoon salt
- ½ teaspoon freshly ground black pepper

NOTE: READY-MADE KIMCHI CAN USUALLY BE FOUND IN THE REFRIGERATED AISLE AT YOUR LOCAL HEALTH FOOD STORE, AT ANY ASIAN GROCER, AND IN SOME SUPERMARKETS.

DIRECTIONS

Preheat the oven to 425°F.

Transfer the kimchi and its juices into the bowl of a food processor, and pulse a few times until very finely chopped (you can also do this manually with a chef's knife; make sure you strain and reserve the juices before chopping the kimchi very finely).

In a bowl, combine the minced kimchi and kimchi juices with the quartered sprouts, olive oil, salt, and pepper. Stir to mix well.

Transfer to a parchment-lined sheet tray and spread out evenly. Roast for 30 minutes, giving the kimchi mixture a stir at the 15-minute mark. The sprouts should look caramelized.

Remove from the oven, set aside to cool, and then transfer the mixture to an airtight container and refrigerate until ready to use. These will keep for up to 7 days.

Crunchies

CANDIED PECANS

MAKES 2½ CUPS (10 PORTIONS)

INGREDIENTS

- ¾ cup firmly packed brown sugar
- ¼ teaspoon ground cinnamon
- ⅛ teaspoon salt
- 1½ cups pecan halves

Here we have two variations for candied pecans: the first is with brown sugar and the second with maple syrup. We tried the maple syrup as a substitution while making the Cabane à Sucre Salad (page 101), and it was just so tasty that we had to provide you the option.

DIRECTIONS

In a heavy-bottomed saucepan, combine the sugar, cinnamon, salt, and 3 tablespoons of water and whisk to combine. Cook over medium heat for 5 minutes until the sugar dissolves and the mixture starts to bubble. Add the pecans, stirring to coat, and cook for an additional 8 to 10 minutes.

Transfer the pecans and their syrup to a parchment-lined sheet tray, spreading out with a spatula to flatten. Allow to cool completely. Use your hands to break into bite-size pieces. Transfer to an airtight container and store at room temperature. These will keep for up to 2 weeks.

MAPLE SYRUP CANDIED PECANS

**MAKES 2½ CUPS
(10 PORTIONS)**

INGREDIENTS

- ¾ cup maple syrup
- ¼ teaspoon ground cinnamon
- ⅛ teaspoon salt
- 1½ cups pecan halves

DIRECTIONS

In a heavy-bottomed saucepan, combine the maple syrup, cinnamon, and salt and whisk to combine. Cook over medium heat for 3 minutes until the syrup starts to bubble. Add the pecans, stirring to coat, and cook for an additional 8 minutes.

Transfer the pecans and their syrup to a parchment-lined sheet tray, spreading out with a spatula to flatten. Allow to cool completely. Use your hands to break into bite-size pieces. Transfer to an airtight container and store at room temperature. These will keep for up to 2 weeks.

CRISPY FRIED SHALLOTS

**MAKES ABOUT 1½ CUPS
(12 PORTIONS)**

INGREDIENTS

- 6 large shallots (about ½ pound)
- 4 cups avocado oil

DIRECTIONS

Peel and slice the shallots into very thin rings using a mandoline or a sharp knife.

Combine the shallots with the avocado oil in a tall, heavy-bottomed saucepan or small Dutch oven.

Heat the oil over medium-high heat. After 3 to 4 minutes, the oil will start to bubble as the shallots release their water. Lower the heat to medium and continue to cook, stirring from time to time, until the shallots are golden brown and the bubbling subsides, about 8 more minutes.

Transfer to a paper towel–lined plate to drain. The shallots will crisp up as they cool. Transfer to an airtight storage container. These will keep for up to 7 days at room temperature.

SPICY PINEAPPLE CRUNCH

**MAKES 2 CUPS
(4 PORTIONS)**

INGREDIENTS

- ¾ cup raw, unsalted peanuts
- 3 cups diced fresh pineapple (½-inch pieces) (about ⅓ pineapple)
- ½ cup lightly packed brown sugar
- Generous ¼ teaspoon red pepper flakes

DIRECTIONS

Preheat the oven to 425°F.

Toast the peanuts on a parchment-lined sheet tray until deep golden brown but not burned, about 5 minutes. Remove from the oven and set aside to cool.

In a bowl, toss the pineapple with the brown sugar and red pepper flakes until evenly coated. Transfer to a parchment-lined sheet tray, and roast for 15 to 20 minutes, until the sugar and the edges of the pineapple start to look caramelized.

Remove from the oven, transfer to a large bowl, roasting juices included, and toss with the toasted peanuts. Transfer to an airtight container and refrigerate until ready to use. This will keep for up to 5 days.

SPICY ROSEMARY NUTS

MAKES 4 CUPS
(16 PORTIONS)

INGREDIENTS

- ¾ cup pecans
- ¾ cup walnuts
- 1 cup cashews
- 1 cup almonds
- 2 tablespoons olive oil
- 2 sprigs rosemary, leaves chopped fine
- ½ teaspoon Cajun Seasoning (page 133)
- ½ teaspoon red pepper flakes
- 2 teaspoons light brown sugar
- 1 teaspoon salt

DIRECTIONS

Preheat the oven to 350°F.

In a large bowl, combine the pecans, walnuts, cashews, and almonds with the olive oil, rosemary, Cajun Seasoning, red pepper flakes, sugar, and salt. Mix well until the nuts are evenly coated.

Spread the nuts on a large sheet tray. Bake for 12 minutes, removing the tray from the oven at the halfway point to turn the nuts, until golden brown. Allow to cool to room temperature. Place in an airtight container and store in a cool place. These will keep for up to 2 months.

HOMEMADE GARLIC AND ROSEMARY PITA CHIPS

MAKES 4 CUPS
(8 PORTIONS)

INGREDIENTS

- 2 thin 6-inch pitas
- 3 tablespoons olive oil
- Salt and freshly ground black pepper
- 1 tablespoon garlic powder
- 1 tablespoon minced rosemary

These were a big hit from our first book and are a welcome addition to many of the fall and winter recipes in this book, so we had to repeat the recipe here. Add these to our Thanksgiving Salad (page 70) (they cling supremely to goat cheese) or, of course, to the Shish Taouk–Inspired Salad (page 87).

DIRECTIONS

Preheat the oven to 375°F. Line a sheet tray with parchment paper.

On a chopping board, cut the pitas into 8 wedges, then pull each wedge apart to form 2 triangles.

Brush each side of the triangles with olive oil, then arrange on the tray. It's okay if the triangles are very close together. Sprinkle generously with salt and pepper, followed by the garlic powder and minced rosemary.

Bake for 5 to 6 minutes, then remove the tray from the oven and turn the chips over. Continue to bake until crisp and golden, another 5 minutes. Remove from the oven and set aside to cool completely. These chips will keep in an airtight container for up to 7 days.

Grains

AMARANTH

**MAKES 2 CUPS
(4 TO 6 PORTIONS)**

INGREDIENTS

- 1½ cups water
- ¼ teaspoon salt
- 1 cup amaranth

DIRECTIONS

In a heavy-bottomed saucepan, bring the water and salt to a boil over medium-high heat. Stir in the amaranth, and when the water returns to a boil, lower the heat, cover, and simmer until the liquid is absorbed, about 20 minutes. Remove from the heat and keep covered for a further 5 minutes. Fluff the amaranth with a fork. Cooked amaranth will keep, refrigerated, in an airtight container for up to 7 days.

BULGUR WHEAT

**MAKES 2 CUPS
(4 TO 6 PORTIONS)**

INGREDIENTS

- 1 cup bulgur wheat
- 2 cups water
- 1 tablespoon olive oil
- ¼ teaspoon salt

DIRECTIONS

In a heavy-bottomed saucepan, combine the bulgur, water, olive oil, and salt. Bring to a boil over medium-high heat. Lower the heat, cover, and simmer for about 12 minutes. Remove from the heat, drain off any excess liquid, and fluff the bulgur with a fork. Cooked bulgur will keep, refrigerated, in an airtight container for up to 7 days.

JASMINE RICE

**MAKES 3 CUPS
(4 TO 6 PORTIONS)**

INGREDIENTS

- 1 cup jasmine rice
- 1¾ cups water
- 1 tablespoon unsalted butter

DIRECTIONS

In a heavy-bottomed saucepan, combine the rice, water, and butter. Bring to a boil over medium-high heat. Cover, turn the heat to the lowest setting, and simmer for 20 minutes. Remove from the heat and keep covered for a further 10 minutes. Fluff the rice with a fork. Cooked rice will keep, refrigerated, in an airtight container for up to 7 days.

LONG-GRAIN RICE

**MAKES 3 CUPS
(4 TO 6 PORTIONS)**

INGREDIENTS

- 1 cup long-grain rice
- 1¾ cups water
- 1 tablespoon unsalted butter

DIRECTIONS

In a heavy-bottomed saucepan, combine the rice, water, and the butter. Bring to a boil over medium-high heat. Cover, turn the heat to the lowest setting, and simmer for 20 minutes. Remove from the heat and keep covered for a further 10 minutes. Fluff the rice with a fork. Cooked rice will keep, refrigerated, in an airtight container for up to 7 days.

PEARL COUSCOUS

MAKES 6 CUPS
(6 PORTIONS)

INGREDIENTS

○ 2½ cups water
○ 2 cups pearl couscous
○ 2 tablespoons olive oil

DIRECTIONS

In a heavy-bottomed saucepan, bring the water to a boil over medium-high heat. Stir in the couscous and the olive oil. When the water returns to a boil, lower the heat almost completely, cover, and simmer for 10 minutes. Remove from the heat and keep covered for a further 5 minutes. Fluff the couscous with a fork. Cooked couscous will keep, refrigerated, in an airtight container for up to 7 days.

QUINOA

MAKES 3 CUPS
(4 TO 6 PORTIONS)

INGREDIENTS

○ 1¾ cups water
○ 1 cup quinoa

DIRECTIONS

In a heavy-bottomed saucepan, bring the water to a boil over medium-high heat. Stir in the quinoa, and when the water returns to a boil, lower the heat, cover, and simmer for 15 minutes. Remove from the heat and keep covered for a further 5 minutes. Fluff the quinoa with a fork. Cooked quinoa will keep, refrigerated, in an airtight container for up to 7 days.

RICE NOODLES

MAKES 6 CUPS
(12 PORTIONS)

INGREDIENTS

○ 1 9-ounce (250 g) package flat rice noodles
○ Sesame oil, as needed

DIRECTIONS

Place the rice noodles in a large mixing bowl.

Bring 8 cups of water to a boil, then pour over the rice noodles and cover completely. Stir the noodles every minute or so to loosen them. When they look and feel limp and tender, 3 to 4 minutes, rinse them under cold water. Drain and toss with a splash of sesame oil to keep the noodles from sticking to each other. These noodles will keep, refrigerated, in an airtight container for up to 5 days.

Spice Mixes

CAJUN SEASONING

MAKES ½ CUP

INGREDIENTS

- 2 tablespoons + 2 teaspoons salt
- 1 tablespoon cayenne
- 1 tablespoon garlic powder
- 1 tablespoon sweet or smoked paprika
- 1 teaspoon onion powder
- 1 teaspoon dried oregano
- 1 teaspoon dried thyme
- 1 teaspoon freshly ground black pepper

This seasoning can be used to spice up Mock Chicken (page 117) and Roasted Marinated Tofu (page 119), and is delicious in Spicy Rosemary Nuts (page 130), used in the Love Salad (page 91). It can elevate any salad with a bit of heat.

DIRECTIONS

Combine all of the ingredients in a small bowl and then transfer to an airtight container until ready to use. This spice blend will keep in a cool, dark place for up to 3 months.

JERK-STYLE SEASONING

MAKES ½ CUP

INGREDIENTS

- 2 tablespoons garlic powder
- 2 tablespoons brown sugar
- 2 tablespoons sweet or smoked paprika
- 2 teaspoons salt
- 2 teaspoons dried thyme
- 1½ teaspoons ground allspice
- ½ teaspoon cayenne

This seasoning is used for our Jerk-Spiced Shrimp (page 97) and Roasted Jerk-Spiced Corn (page 126) and is a key ingredient in our Tropical Avocado Dressing (page 138).

DIRECTIONS

In a small bowl, combine all of the spices. Store in an airtight container in a cool, dark place for up to 6 months.

Dressings

★ CHAPTER THREE ★

SWEET TAMARI

MAKES 1 CUP (250 ML)

INGREDIENTS

- Scant ½ cup (100 ml) sunflower oil
- 1 tablespoon toasted sesame oil
- ¼ cup (60 ml) agave syrup
- 2 tablespoons tamari
- ½ cup (125 ml) apple cider vinegar
- 1 clove garlic
- ¼ cup packed (13 g) nutritional yeast flakes
- ½ cup + 1 tablespoon (135 ml) olive oil
- Salt and freshly ground black pepper

DIRECTIONS

In a blender, combine the sunflower oil, sesame oil, agave syrup, tamari, vinegar, garlic, and nutritional yeast. Process on medium-high speed until smooth and well combined, 20 to 30 seconds. Stop the blender and scrape down the sides of the jar with a spatula as needed.

With the blender running on low speed, slowly drizzle in the olive oil until the dressing is emulsified and thickened, about 30 seconds. Season to taste with salt and pepper. Transfer the dressing to an airtight container and refrigerate until ready to use.

This dressing will keep, refrigerated, for up to 7 days.

SMOOTH SESAME

MAKES 2 CUPS (500 ML)

INGREDIENTS

- ¼ cup (60 ml) mayonnaise
- 1 teaspoon wasabi paste or powder
- 2 teaspoons granulated sugar
- 1 clove garlic, minced
- 2 tablespoons minced red onion
- ⅓ cup (80 ml) tamari
- ⅓ cup (80 ml) rice vinegar
- 3 tablespoons mirin
- 1 teaspoon sesame oil
- ¾ cup (180 ml) avocado or sunflower oil

DIRECTIONS

In a blender, combine the mayonnaise, wasabi, sugar, garlic, onion, tamari, rice vinegar, and mirin. Process on medium-high speed until smooth and well combined, 15 to 20 seconds. Stop the blender and scrape down the sides of the jar with a spatula as needed.

With the blender running on low speed, add the sesame oil and slowly drizzle in the avocado oil until the dressing is emulsified and thickened, about 30 seconds. Transfer the dressing to an airtight container and refrigerate until ready to use.

This dressing will keep, refrigerated, for up to 7 days.

RANCH

MAKES 2 CUPS (500 ML)

INGREDIENTS

- Generous ¾ cup (200 ml) whole milk
- 1 teaspoon lemon juice
- 1 teaspoon apple cider vinegar
- 1 cup (250 ml) mayonnaise
- 1 teaspoon whole-grain mustard
- 1 teaspoon garlic powder
- 1 teaspoon onion powder
- ¼ cup (60 ml) olive oil
- 1 teaspoon salt
- ½ teaspoon freshly ground black pepper
- ¼ cup (15 g) minced chives
- ¼ cup (15 g) minced flat-leaf parsley
- 2 teaspoons minced red onion (optional)

DIRECTIONS

In a small bowl, whisk together the milk, lemon juice, and vinegar and set aside to curdle at room temperature, about 10 minutes.

In a blender, combine the soured milk with the mayonnaise, mustard, and garlic and onion powders. Process on medium-high speed until smooth and well combined, 15 to 20 seconds. Stop the blender and scrape down the sides of the jar with a spatula as needed.

With the blender running on low speed, slowly drizzle in the olive oil until the dressing is emulsified and thickened, about 30 seconds. Add the salt and pepper, adjusting the seasoning to taste.

Transfer the dressing to an airtight container, then stir in the minced herbs and red onion and refrigerate until ready to use.

This dressing will keep, refrigerated, for up to 7 days.

BLUE RANCH 2.0

MAKES 2 CUPS (500 ML)

INGREDIENTS

- 1 cup (120 g) crumbled blue cheese
- ½ cup (125 ml) sour cream
- ⅓ cup (80 ml) mayonnaise
- 6 tablespoons (90 ml) milk or buttermilk
- 1 tablespoon horseradish cream
- 1½ tablespoons apple cider vinegar
- 1 teaspoon Tabasco
- 2 teaspoons lime juice
- ¼ teaspoon salt
- ½ teaspoon freshly ground black pepper
- 2 tablespoons minced chives

DIRECTIONS

In a blender, combine all of the ingredients except for the salt, pepper, and chives. Process on medium-high speed until smooth and well combined, 15 to 20 seconds. Stop the blender and scrape down the sides of the jar with a spatula as needed.

Add the salt and pepper, adjusting the seasoning to taste, followed by the chives. Transfer the dressing to an airtight container and refrigerate until ready to use.

This dressing will keep, refrigerated, for up to 7 days.

AVOCADO

MAKES 2 CUPS (500 ML)

INGREDIENTS

- 1 large ripe avocado
- 1 scallion, sliced
- 1 clove garlic, minced
- 1 teaspoon sambal oelek
- ½ cup (125 ml) orange juice
- ¼ cup (60 ml) apple cider vinegar
- ½ cup (125 ml) avocado oil
- 1 teaspoon salt
- ½ teaspoon freshly ground black pepper

NOTE: SAMBAL OELEK IS AN INDONESIAN CHILI PASTE THAT CAN BE FOUND AT MOST GROCERY STORES.

DIRECTIONS

In a blender, combine the avocado, scallion, garlic, sambal oelek, orange juice, and vinegar. Process on medium-high speed until smooth and well combined, 15 to 20 seconds. Stop the blender and scrape down the sides of the jar with a spatula as needed.

With the blender running on low speed, slowly drizzle in the avocado oil until the dressing is emulsified and thickened, about 30 seconds. Add the salt and pepper, adjusting the seasoning to taste. Transfer the dressing to an airtight container and refrigerate until ready to use.

This dressing will keep, refrigerated, for up to 3 days.

TROPICAL AVOCADO

MAKES 2 CUPS (500 ML)

INGREDIENTS

- 1 large ripe avocado
- ¼ cup (60 ml) lime juice
- ½ teaspoon red pepper flakes
- 1 tablespoon Jerk-Style Seasoning (page 133)
- Scant ½ cup (100 ml) Sweet Sesame Syrup (see below)
- 1 cup + 2 tablespoons (280 ml) olive oil
- ½ teaspoon salt
- ¼ teaspoon freshly ground black pepper

DIRECTIONS

In a blender, combine the avocado, lime juice, red pepper flakes, Jerk-Style Seasoning, and Sweet Sesame Syrup. Process on medium-high speed until smooth and well combined, 15 to 20 seconds. Stop the blender and scrape down the sides of the jar with a spatula as needed.

With the blender running on low speed, slowly drizzle in the olive oil until the dressing is emulsified and thickened, about 30 seconds. Add the salt and pepper, adjusting the seasoning to taste. Transfer the dressing to an airtight container and refrigerate until ready to use.

This dressing will keep, refrigerated, for up to 7 days.

SWEET SESAME SYRUP

MAKES 1¼ CUPS (300 ML)

INGREDIENTS

- ¾ cup (180 ml) agave syrup
- ½ cup (125 ml) apple cider vinegar
- 3 tablespoons tamari

DIRECTIONS

In a small saucepan, combine the agave syrup and vinegar. Over medium heat, whisking well, bring to a simmer. Remove from the heat and stir in the tamari.

This dressing will keep, refrigerated, for up to 3 days.

GINGER LIME

MAKES 2 CUPS (500 ML)

INGREDIENTS

- ⅓ cup (35 g) coarsely chopped ginger
- 1 clove garlic, minced
- ¼ cup (45 g) firmly packed brown sugar
- ¼ teaspoon red pepper flakes
- ¾ cup (180 ml) lime juice
- 3 tablespoons tamari
- 3 tablespoons toasted sesame oil
- ½ cup + 1 tablespoon (135 ml) olive oil
- ½ teaspoon salt
- ¼ teaspoon freshly ground black pepper

DIRECTIONS

In a blender, combine the ginger, garlic, sugar, red pepper flakes, lime juice, and tamari. Process on medium-high speed until completely smooth and well combined, 15 to 20 seconds. Stop the blender and scrape down the sides of the jar with a spatula as needed.

With the blender running on low speed, slowly drizzle in the sesame oil, followed by the olive oil, until the dressing is emulsified, about 30 seconds. Add the salt and pepper, adjusting the seasoning to taste. Transfer the dressing to an airtight container and refrigerate until ready to use.

This dressing will keep, refrigerated, for up to 7 days.

LEMON THYME

MAKES 2 CUPS (500 ML)

INGREDIENTS

- 2 teaspoons Dijon mustard
- 1 clove garlic, minced
- ⅓ cup (80 ml) lemon juice
- ⅓ cup (80 ml) apple cider vinegar
- ⅓ cup (80 ml) simple syrup
- 1¼ cups (310 ml) olive oil
- Zest of 2 lemons
- 2 tablespoons thyme leaves
- ½ teaspoon salt
- 1 teaspoon freshly ground black pepper

NOTE: MAKE SURE YOU ZEST THE TWO LEMONS BEFORE YOU SQUEEZE THEM FOR THEIR JUICE—IT'S MUCH HARDER TO ZEST A JUICED LEMON HALF! IF YOU DON'T HAVE SIMPLE SYRUP ON HAND, JUST BOIL 1 CUP OF WATER WITH 1 CUP OF SUGAR UNTIL DISSOLVED, LET COOL, THEN MEASURE OUT ⅓ CUP. THE REMAINDER CAN BE KEPT IN AN AIRTIGHT CONTAINER AT ROOM TEMPERATURE FOR A LONG TIME.

DIRECTIONS

In a blender, combine the mustard, garlic, lemon juice, vinegar, and simple syrup. Process on medium-high speed until smooth and well combined, 15 to 20 seconds. Stop the blender and scrape down the sides of the jar with a spatula as needed.

With the blender running on low speed, slowly drizzle in the olive oil until the dressing is emulsified and thickened, about 30 seconds. Add the lemon zest, thyme, salt, and pepper, adjusting the seasoning to taste. Transfer the dressing to an airtight container and refrigerate until ready to use.

This dressing will keep, refrigerated, for up to 7 days.

POMEGRANATE

MAKES 2 CUPS (500 ML)

INGREDIENTS

- ¼ cup (60 ml) apple cider vinegar
- ¾ cup (180 ml) pomegranate juice
- ⅓ cup (70 g) granulated sugar
- 1 tablespoon lemon juice
- 1 tablespoon Dijon mustard
- ½ cup (125 ml) olive oil
- ½ teaspoon salt
- ½ teaspoon freshly ground black pepper

DIRECTIONS

In a small saucepan, combine the vinegar, pomegranate juice, and sugar. Bring to a boil over medium-high heat and whisk to dissolve the sugar. Set aside to cool.

In a blender, combine the cooled pomegranate syrup, lemon juice, and mustard. Process on medium-high speed until smooth and well combined, 15 to 20 seconds. Stop the blender and scrape down the sides of the jar with a spatula as needed.

With the blender running on low speed, slowly drizzle in the olive oil until the dressing is emulsified and thickened, about 30 seconds. Add the salt and pepper, adjusting the seasoning to taste. Transfer the dressing to an airtight container and refrigerate until ready to use.

This dressing will keep, refrigerated, for up to 7 days.

AUTUMN ALMOND

MAKES 2 CUPS (500 ML)

INGREDIENTS

- ½ cup (125 ml) almond butter
- Zest of 1 lemon
- 3 tablespoons lemon juice
- 1 tablespoon red wine vinegar
- 1 clove coarsely chopped garlic
- ½ cup (125 ml) olive oil
- ½ cup (125 ml) avocado oil
- ½ teaspoon salt
- ½ teaspoon freshly ground black pepper

DIRECTIONS

In a blender, combine the almond butter, lemon zest, lemon juice, vinegar, and garlic. Process on medium-high speed until combined, 15 to 20 seconds. Stop the blender and scrape down the sides of the jar with a spatula as needed.

With the blender running on low speed, slowly drizzle in the olive and avocado oils until the mixture thickens, about 30 seconds. It may look lumpy and grainy! With the blender still running, slowly pour in ½ cup of water, and keep blending until the mixture is smooth. You may need to add a splash more water to loosen the consistency of the dressing to your liking. Add the salt and pepper, adjusting the seasoning to taste. Transfer the dressing to an airtight container and refrigerate until ready to use.

This dressing will keep, refrigerated, for up to 7 days.

THAI CHILI AND MISO

MAKES 2 CUPS (500 ML)

INGREDIENTS

- ⅓ cup (90 g) red miso
- ⅓ cup (60 g) lightly packed brown sugar
- ⅓ cup (80 ml) honey
- ¼ cup (60 ml) fish sauce
- 2 tablespoons tamari
- 5 tablespoons (75 ml) lime juice
- 1 teaspoon minced Thai chili
- Scant ½ cup (105 ml) avocado oil
- 2 teaspoons freshly ground black pepper
- Salt

DIRECTIONS

In a blender, combine the miso, brown sugar, honey, fish sauce, tamari, lime juice, Thai chili, and 3 tablespoons of warm water. Process on medium-high speed until smooth and well combined, 15 to 20 seconds. Stop the blender and scrape down the sides of the jar with a spatula as needed.

With the blender running on low speed, slowly drizzle in the avocado oil until the dressing is emulsified and thickened, about 30 seconds. Add the pepper and salt to taste, adjusting the seasoning to your liking. Transfer the dressing to an airtight container and refrigerate until ready to use.

This dressing will keep, refrigerated, for up to 3 days.

SUNSHINE

MAKES 2 CUPS (500 ML)

INGREDIENTS

- 3 tablespoons coarsely chopped ginger
- 2 cloves garlic, coarsely chopped
- ¾ cup (180 ml) lemon juice
- 2 tablespoons maple syrup
- 2 teaspoons Dijon mustard
- 2 teaspoons toasted sesame oil
- 1 teaspoon ground turmeric
- ⅛ teaspoon cayenne
- 1¼ cups (300 ml) olive oil
- Fine sea salt and freshly ground black pepper

DIRECTIONS

In a blender, combine the ginger, garlic, lemon juice, maple syrup, mustard, sesame oil, turmeric, and cayenne. Process on medium-high speed until smooth and well combined, 15 to 20 seconds. Stop the blender and scrape down the sides of the jar with a spatula as needed.

With the blender running on low speed, slowly drizzle in the olive oil until the dressing is emulsified and thickened, about 30 seconds. Add salt and pepper, adjusting the seasoning to taste. Transfer the dressing to an airtight container and refrigerate until ready to use.

This dressing will keep, refrigerated, for up to 7 days.

PARMESAN

MAKES 2 CUPS (500 ML)

INGREDIENTS

- 1 large egg
- 1 clove garlic, coarsely chopped
- ½ cup (125 ml) best-quality red wine vinegar
- 1½ cups (150 g) freshly grated Parmesan
- 1⅓ cups (305 ml) olive oil
- ½ teaspoon salt
- ½ teaspoon freshly ground black pepper

NOTE: WE DON'T KNOW HOW TO SAY THIS, UM, TASTEFULLY, BUT IF YOU USE STALE SUPERMARKET PRE-GRATED PARM AND CHEAPO VINEGAR, THE DRESSING WON'T BE SMOOTH OR BALANCED, AND IT WON'T TASTE GREAT. THIS DRESSING REALLY DEPENDS ON HIGH-QUALITY INGREDIENTS FOR A FANTASTIC FINAL RESULT. SO ONLY PROCEED WHEN YOU'RE WILLING TO SPEND ON A BLOCK OF GOOD-QUALITY PARMESAN CHEESE, BECAUSE WE WANT YOU TO HAVE THE BEST RESULT.

DIRECTIONS

In a blender, combine the egg, garlic, vinegar, and Parmesan. Process on medium-high speed until smooth and well combined, 15 to 20 seconds. Stop the blender and scrape down the sides of the jar with a spatula as needed.

With the blender running on low speed, slowly drizzle in the olive oil until the dressing is emulsified and thickened, about 30 seconds. Add the salt and pepper, adjusting the seasoning to taste. Transfer the dressing to an airtight container and refrigerate until ready to use.

This dressing will keep, refrigerated, for up to 3 days.

SAGE AND ROSEMARY

MAKES 2 CUPS (500 ML)

INGREDIENTS

- ¼ cup (60 ml) apple cider vinegar
- 1 tablespoon honey
- 1 tablespoon Dijon mustard
- 2 cloves garlic, minced
- ½ cup (7 g) basil leaves
- ¼ cup (5 g) sage leaves
- 2 tablespoons rosemary leaves
- Scant ⅔ cup (150 ml) olive oil
- ¼ teaspoon salt
- ½ teaspoon freshly ground black pepper

DIRECTIONS

In a blender, combine the vinegar, honey, mustard, garlic, basil, sage, and rosemary. Process on medium-high speed until smooth and well combined, 15 to 20 seconds. Stop the blender and scrape down the sides of the jar with a spatula as needed.

With the blender running on low speed, slowly drizzle in the olive oil until the dressing is emulsified and thickened, about 30 seconds. Add the salt and pepper, adjusting the seasoning to taste. Transfer the dressing to an airtight container and refrigerate until ready to use.

This dressing will keep, refrigerated, for up to 3 days.

CRANBERRY

MAKES 2 CUPS (500 ML)

INGREDIENTS

- 1½ cups (375 ml) Cranberry–Red Onion Jam (see below)
- 1 tablespoon Dijon mustard
- ½ cup (125 ml) olive oil
- Salt and freshly ground black pepper

NOTE: THIS RECIPE INCLUDES MAKING A BATCH OF CRANBERRY–RED ONION JAM, BUT YOU CAN SUBSTITUTE YOUR FAVORITE STORE-BOUGHT SAUCE OR, OF COURSE, ANY LEFTOVER CRANBERRY SAUCE FROM THANKSGIVING OR CHRISTMAS!

DIRECTIONS

In a blender, combine the Cranberry–Red Onion Jam with the Dijon mustard. Process on medium-high speed until smooth and well combined, 15 to 20 seconds. Stop the blender and scrape down the sides of the jar with a spatula as needed.

With the blender running on low speed, slowly drizzle in the olive oil until the dressing is emulsified and thickened, about 30 seconds. Add salt and pepper, adjusting the seasoning to taste. Transfer the dressing to an airtight container and refrigerate until ready to use.

This dressing will keep, refrigerated, for up to 7 days.

CRANBERRY–RED ONION JAM

MAKES 1½ CUPS (375 ML)

INGREDIENTS

- 1 tablespoon olive oil
- 1 cup (150 g) finely sliced red onion
- 1 teaspoon minced rosemary
- 1 teaspoon thyme leaves
- 2 cups (200 g) cranberries (frozen or fresh)
- ½ cup (125 ml) red wine vinegar
- ½ cup (100 g) granulated sugar

DIRECTIONS

In a heavy-bottomed saucepan, warm the olive oil over medium heat. Add the onion, rosemary, and thyme and cook gently until the onions are translucent, about 5 minutes. Stir in the cranberries, vinegar, and sugar and bring to a boil over medium-high heat.

Lower the heat and simmer for 25 minutes, until the cranberries have softened and the liquid has turned syrupy. Remove from the heat and allow the mixture to cool to lukewarm.

Transfer the mixture to the blender and blend until smooth. Transfer to an airtight container and refrigerate until ready to use.

This jam will keep, refrigerated, for up to 2 months.

KEWPIE

MAKES 2 CUPS (500 ML)

INGREDIENTS

- 1½ tablespoons karashi
- 3 tablespoons Kewpie mayonnaise
- ½ cup (125 ml) tamari
- ⅓ cup (80 ml) seasoned rice vinegar
- 3 tablespoons mirin
- 1 teaspoon toasted sesame oil
- 1 teaspoon granulated sugar
- 1 clove garlic, coarsely chopped
- ½ cup (125 ml) avocado oil
- Salt and freshly ground black pepper

NOTE: YOU'LL FIND KARASHI (JAPANESE MUSTARD), KEWPIE MAYONNAISE, MIRIN (JAPANESE SWEET COOKING WINE), AND RICE VINEGAR AT ANY ASIAN GROCERY STORE.

DIRECTIONS

In a blender, combine the karashi, mayonnaise, tamari, vinegar, mirin, sesame oil, sugar, and garlic. Process on medium-high speed until smooth and well combined, 15 to 20 seconds. Stop the blender and scrape down the sides of the jar with a spatula as needed.

With the blender running on low speed, slowly drizzle in the avocado oil until the dressing is emulsified and thickened, about 30 seconds. Add the salt and pepper, adjusting the seasoning to taste. Transfer the dressing to an airtight container and refrigerate until ready to use.

This dressing will keep, refrigerated, for up to 7 days.

MORINGA

MAKES 2 CUPS (500 ML)

INGREDIENTS

- 3 tablespoons moringa powder
- ⅓ cup (80 ml) apple cider vinegar
- ¼ cup (60 ml) maple syrup
- ⅓ cup + 2 teaspoons (90 ml) lime juice
- 1 cup (250 ml) avocado oil
- 2 cloves garlic, minced
- 1 teaspoon salt
- 1 teaspoon freshly ground black pepper

NOTE: MORINGA LEAF ORIGINATES FROM INDIA AND HAS BEEN USED IN TRADITIONAL MEDICINE FOR CENTURIES. IT IS RICH IN ANTIOXIDANTS AND NUTRIENTS, AND YOU CAN FIND IT AT ANY HEALTH FOOD STORE. MORINGA IS THE DEFINING FLAVOR OF THIS DRESSING. IT'S AWESOME IN A KIND OF MATCHA-FEELING WAY.

DIRECTIONS

In a blender, combine the moringa powder, vinegar, maple syrup, and lime juice. Process on medium-high speed until smooth and well combined, 15 to 20 seconds. Stop the blender and scrape down the sides of the jar with a spatula as needed.

With the blender running on low speed, slowly drizzle in the avocado oil until the dressing is emulsified and thickened, about 30 seconds. Add the garlic, salt, and pepper, adjusting the seasoning to taste. Transfer the dressing to an airtight container and refrigerate until ready to use.

This dressing will keep, refrigerated, for up to 7 days.

LEVANTINE

MAKES 2 CUPS (500 ML)

INGREDIENTS

- ½ cup (125 ml) plain yogurt
- ½ cup (125 ml) mayonnaise
- Zest and juice of 1 lemon (3 tablespoons)
- 2 cloves garlic, minced
- 1 teaspoon sumac
- 3 tablespoons sesame seeds
- ¼ cup (7 g) coarsely chopped mint leaves (packed)
- ½ teaspoon dried thyme
- ½ teaspoon dried oregano
- ½ cup (125 ml) olive oil
- ½ teaspoon salt
- ¼ teaspoon freshly ground black pepper

DIRECTIONS

In a blender, combine the yogurt, mayonnaise, lemon juice and zest, garlic, sumac, and sesame seeds. Process on medium-high speed until smooth and well combined, 15 to 20 seconds. Stop the blender and scrape down the sides of the jar with a spatula as needed. Add the mint, thyme, and oregano and blend just to combine, 2 to 3 seconds.

With the blender running on low speed, slowly drizzle in the olive oil until the dressing is emulsified and thickened, about 30 seconds. Add the salt and pepper, adjusting the seasoning to taste. Transfer the dressing to an airtight container and refrigerate until ready to use.

This dressing will keep, refrigerated, for up to 7 days.

CREAMY GINGER MINT

MAKES 2 CUPS (500 ML)

INGREDIENTS

- ½ cup (125 ml) mayonnaise
- ¾ cup (180 ml) plain yogurt
- 1 cup (28 g) mint leaves
- ½ cup (50 g) thinly sliced scallions
- ½ cup (50 g) coarsely chopped ginger
- Zest and juice of 1 lime
- 1 tablespoon honey
- 1 teaspoon salt
- 1 teaspoon freshly ground black pepper

DIRECTIONS

In a blender, combine the mayonnaise, yogurt, mint, scallions, ginger, lime zest and juice, and honey. Process on medium-high speed until smooth and well combined, 15 to 20 seconds. Stop the blender and scrape down the sides of the jar with a spatula as needed.

Add the salt and pepper, adjusting the seasoning to taste. Transfer the dressing to an airtight container and refrigerate until ready to use.

This dressing will keep, refrigerated, for up to 3 days.

VERY BERRY

MAKES 2 CUPS (500 ML)

INGREDIENTS

- ¼ cup (40 g) frozen blueberries
- ¼ cup (40 g) frozen raspberries
- ¼ cup (35 g) frozen strawberries
- 2 tablespoons honey
- 1 clove garlic
- ⅓ cup (80 ml) apple cider vinegar
- Scant 1 cup (210 ml) olive oil
- 1 cup (14 g) basil leaves
- ½ teaspoon salt
- ¼ teaspoon freshly ground black pepper

DIRECTIONS

In a blender, combine the blueberries, raspberries, strawberries, honey, garlic, and vinegar. Process on medium-high speed until smooth and well combined, 15 to 20 seconds. Stop the blender and scrape down the sides of the jar with a spatula as needed.

With the blender running on low speed, slowly drizzle in the olive oil until the dressing is emulsified and thickened, about 30 seconds. Add the basil, salt, and pepper, and blend to combine, 7 to 10 seconds.

Transfer the dressing to an airtight container and refrigerate until ready to use.

This dressing will keep, refrigerated, for up to 3 days.

SPICY MAPLE

MAKES 2 CUPS (500 ML)

INGREDIENTS

- 2 cloves garlic
- 6 tablespoons (90 ml) apple cider vinegar
- ¼ cup (60 ml) maple syrup
- 1 tablespoon Dijon mustard
- 1¼ cups (300 ml) olive oil
- ½ teaspoon salt
- 1½ teaspoons freshly ground black pepper

DIRECTIONS

In a blender, combine the garlic, vinegar, maple syrup, and mustard. Process on medium-high speed until smooth and well combined, 15 to 20 seconds. Stop the blender and scrape down the sides of the jar with a spatula as needed.

With the blender running on low speed, slowly drizzle in the olive oil until the dressing is emulsified and thickened, about 30 seconds. Add the salt and pepper, adjusting the seasoning to taste. Transfer the dressing to an airtight container and refrigerate until ready to use.

This dressing will keep, refrigerated, for up to 7 days.

ÉPIS-STYLE

MAKES 2 CUPS (500 ML)

INGREDIENTS

- 1 cup (250 ml) Épis-Style Seasoning (see below)
- 1 tablespoon Dijon mustard
- 2 tablespoons maple syrup
- ½ cup (100 g) coarsely chopped pineapple
- ⅓ cup (80 ml) olive oil
- Salt and freshly ground black pepper

NOTE: ÉPIS (PRONOUNCED "AY-PEACE," AND A HOMONYM OF THE FRENCH WORD FOR "SPICE") IS A BLEND OF BELL PEPPERS, HOT PEPPERS, ONIONS, GARLIC, PARSLEY, AND VARIOUS SPICES, AND IS THE FOUNDATION OF MANY DISHES FROM HAITI. THE ÉPIS-STYLE SEASONING BASE USED IN THIS DRESSING CAN ALSO BE USED TO SEASON MEATS, SOUPS, RICE DISHES, AND MORE.

DIRECTIONS

In a blender, combine the épis-style seasoning, mustard, maple syrup, and pineapple. Process on medium-high speed until smooth and well combined, 15 to 20 seconds. Stop the blender and scrape down the sides of the jar with a spatula as needed.

With the blender running on low speed, slowly drizzle in the oil until the dressing is emulsified and thickened, about 30 seconds. Add the salt and pepper, adjusting the seasoning to taste. Transfer the dressing to an airtight container and refrigerate until ready to use.

This dressing will keep, refrigerated, for up to 7 days.

ÉPIS-STYLE SEASONING

MAKES ABOUT 2 CUPS (500 ML)

INGREDIENTS

- ½ small red bell pepper, coarsely chopped
- ½ small yellow bell pepper, coarsely chopped
- ½ small green bell pepper, coarsely chopped
- 1 stalk celery, coarsely chopped
- 3 scallions, coarsely chopped
- 2 tablespoons finely chopped red onion
- 1 large jalapeño pepper, seeded and minced
- 1 cup (50 g) packed flat-leaf parsley (stems and leaves)
- 6 cloves garlic, minced
- ¼ cup (60 ml) olive or canola oil
- 1 tablespoon thyme leaves
- 1½ teaspoons salt

DIRECTIONS

In a blender or food processor, combine the bell peppers, celery, scallions, red onion, jalapeño, parsley, and garlic. Process on medium-high speed until smooth and well combined, 15 to 20 seconds. Stop the blender and scrape down the sides of the jar with a spatula as needed.

With the blender running on low speed, slowly drizzle in the oil until the mixture has thickened to a paste or sauce-like consistency, about 30 seconds. You may need to add a splash of water or oil to help the paste come together. Add the thyme and salt, adjusting the seasoning to taste. Transfer the mixture to an airtight container and refrigerate until ready to use.

This seasoning will keep, refrigerated, for up to 5 days.

SPICY SRIRACHA

MAKES 2 CUPS (500 ML)

INGREDIENTS

- ¼ cup + 1 tablespoon (75 ml) mayonnaise
- ½ cup (50 g) freshly grated Parmesan
- ¼ cup (60 ml) red wine vinegar
- 1 tablespoon lemon juice
- 1 clove garlic, minced
- 3 tablespoons Smoke Show lightly smoked jalapeño hot sauce
- 3 tablespoons Sriracha sauce
- 1 tablespoon Dijon mustard
- ¾ cup (180 ml) olive oil
- ½ teaspoon salt
- ¼ teaspoon freshly ground black pepper

NOTE: THIS DRESSING IS DESIGNED FOR OUR SPICY MEAT SALAD (PAGE 102) BUT COULD EASILY—AND DELICIOUSLY—BE USED FOR DRIZZLING ONTO YOUR FAVORITE MEAT (OR MEATLESS) SUB!

DIRECTIONS

In a blender, combine the mayonnaise, Parmesan, vinegar, lemon juice, garlic, hot sauce, Sriracha, and mustard. Process on medium-high speed until smooth and well combined, 15 to 20 seconds. Stop the blender and scrape down the sides of the jar with a spatula as needed.

With the blender running on low speed, slowly drizzle in the olive oil until the dressing is emulsified and thickened, about 30 seconds. Add the salt and pepper, adjusting the seasoning to taste. Transfer the dressing to an airtight container and refrigerate until ready to use.

This dressing will keep, refrigerated, for up to 7 days.

BASEBALL MUSTARD

MAKES 2 CUPS (500 ML)

INGREDIENTS

- ¾ cup (180 ml) yellow mustard
- 1 tablespoon Dijon mustard
- ⅓ cup (80 ml) mayonnaise
- 2 tablespoons olive oil
- ¼ cup (60 ml) red wine vinegar
- 1 tablespoon lemon juice
- 1 clove garlic, minced
- 1 cup (100 g) freshly grated Parmesan
- ½ teaspoon salt
- ½ teaspoon freshly ground black pepper

DIRECTIONS

In a blender, combine the yellow mustard, Dijon mustard, mayonnaise, olive oil, vinegar, lemon juice and garlic. Process on medium-high speed until smooth and well combined, 15 to 20 seconds. Stop the blender and scrape down the sides of the jar with a spatula as needed.

Add the Parmesan and run the blender on low speed to combine. Add the salt and pepper, adjusting the seasoning to taste. Transfer the dressing to an airtight container and refrigerate until ready to use.

This dressing will keep, refrigerated, for up to 7 days.

LEMON CINNAMON

MAKES 2 CUPS (500 ML)

INGREDIENTS

- ¼ cup (25 g) coarsely chopped ginger
- 2 tablespoons Dijon mustard
- ½ cup (125 ml) agave syrup
- ⅓ cup (80 ml) lemon juice
- ⅓ cup (80 ml apple cider vinegar
- 1 tablespoon ground cinnamon
- ½ cup (125 ml) olive oil
- 1 teaspoon salt
- ¼ teaspoon freshly ground black pepper

DIRECTIONS

In a blender, combine the ginger, mustard, agave syrup, lemon juice, vinegar, and cinnamon. Process on medium-high speed until smooth and well combined, 15 to 20 seconds. Stop the blender and scrape down the sides of the jar with a spatula as needed.

With the blender running on low speed, slowly drizzle in the olive oil until the dressing is emulsified and thickened, about 30 seconds. Add the salt and pepper, adjusting the seasoning to taste. Transfer the dressing to an airtight container and refrigerate until ready to use.

This dressing will keep, refrigerated, for up to 7 days.

MISO GINGER

MAKES 2 CUPS (500 ML)

INGREDIENTS

- ¼ cup (60 g) white miso
- ½ cup (60 g) coarsely chopped ginger
- 1 tablespoon Sriracha sauce
- ½ cup (125 ml) rice vinegar
- 1 tablespoon lime juice
- 3 tablespoons agave syrup
- ⅓ cup (80 ml) tamari
- 1 tablespoon sesame oil
- ¼ cup (60 ml) olive oil
- Salt and freshly ground black pepper

DIRECTIONS

In a blender, combine the miso, ginger, Sriracha, rice vinegar, lime juice, agave syrup, and tamari. Process on medium-high speed until smooth and well combined, 15 to 20 seconds. Stop the blender and scrape down the sides of the jar with a spatula as needed.

With the blender running on low speed, slowly drizzle in the sesame oil, followed by the olive oil, until the dressing is emulsified and thickened, about 30 seconds. Add the salt and pepper, adjusting the seasoning to taste. Transfer the dressing to an airtight container and refrigerate until ready to use.

This dressing will keep, refrigerated, for up to 7 days.

SATAY

MAKES 2 CUPS (500 ML)

INGREDIENTS

- Scant ½ cup (100 ml) sunflower oil
- 1 tablespoon toasted sesame oil
- ¼ cup (60 ml) agave syrup
- 3 tablespoons apple cider vinegar
- 1 tablespoon tamari
- 1 cup (20 g) packed cilantro leaves
- 3 tablespoons lime juice
- 3 tablespoons honey or agave syrup
- 3 tablespoons coarsely chopped ginger
- 3 cloves garlic, minced
- ½ cup (125 ml) olive oil
- ½ teaspoon salt
- ¼ teaspoon freshly ground black pepper

DIRECTIONS

Pour the sunflower oil, sesame oil, agave syrup, vinegar, and tamari into a bowl and whisk well to combine. Set aside.

In a blender, combine the cilantro, lime juice, honey, ginger, and garlic. Blend until coarsely chopped and combined, 15 to 20 seconds. Stop the blender and scrape down the sides of the jar with a spatula as needed.

Add the sesame-tamari mixture to the blender and give things a quick spin to combine. Transfer the dressing to an airtight container and refrigerate until ready to use.

This dressing will keep, refrigerated, for up to 3 days.

NIÇOISE

MAKES 2 CUPS (500 ML)

INGREDIENTS

- 2 anchovy fillets, with some of their oil reserved
- 2 tablespoons whole-grain mustard
- 1 teaspoon granulated sugar
- ½ cup (125 ml) lemon juice
- 1½ cups (375 ml) olive oil
- 1 shallot, minced
- ½ teaspoon salt
- ¼ teaspoon freshly ground black pepper

NOTE: YOU CAN USE SOME OIL FROM THE ANCHOVIES AND/OR THE CANNED TUNA YOU'RE USING FOR THE TUNA PROVENÇALE SALAD (PAGE 54) AS PART OF THE OIL IN THE DRESSING.

DIRECTIONS

In a blender, combine the anchovies, mustard, sugar, and lemon juice. Process on medium-high speed until smooth and well combined, 15 to 20 seconds. Stop the blender and scrape down the sides of the jar with a spatula as needed.

With the blender running on low speed, slowly drizzle in the olive oil until the dressing is emulsified and thickened, about 30 seconds. Add the shallot, followed by the salt and pepper, adjusting the seasoning to taste. Transfer the dressing to an airtight container and refrigerate until ready to use.

This dressing will keep, refrigerated, for up to 7 days.

Soups

★ CHAPTER FOUR ★

Quinoa Veggie Chili

∘ MAKES 6 CUPS (4 PORTIONS) ∘

Picture the scene: it's 2009, we're in our tiny kitchen on Avenue Laurier (at the back of Mimi & Coco clothing store), it's winter, sales are dwindling as they always did in winter months, and it's COLD. We look around and spot the little single plug-in element we use to cook the quinoa for some of our salads. Then, after considering the ingredients we have on hand, it hits us: "What if we try making homemade chili for our guests during the colder months?" And voilà, the first of our in-house soups is born!

INGREDIENTS

- 3 tablespoons olive oil
- 1 small onion, diced small
- 2 cloves garlic, minced
- 2 teaspoons ground cumin
- ¼ teaspoon crushed red pepper flakes
- Salt and freshly ground black pepper
- 1 small red bell pepper, diced small
- 1 small green bell pepper, diced small
- 1 small zucchini, diced small
- 1 14-ounce (398 ml) can diced tomatoes
- 1 cup low-sodium vegetable broth
- ¾ cup corn kernels
- ¾ cup red kidney beans
- ¾ cup black beans
- 1½ cups Quinoa (page 132)
- ¼ cup minced cilantro
- 2 cups blue corn tortilla chips
- Cilantro leaves, for garnish

DIRECTIONS

In a Dutch oven, warm the olive oil over medium-low heat. Add the onion and garlic and cook, stirring occasionally, until the onions soften and become translucent, about 5 minutes. Stir in the cumin and red pepper flakes and season lightly with salt and pepper. Add the red and green pepper, zucchini, canned tomatoes, and most of the broth to the pot and bring to a boil. Lower the heat completely and simmer for 10 minutes.

Stir in the corn, kidney beans, black beans, cooked quinoa, and minced cilantro and continue to simmer for about 2 minutes. Add a splash more broth if needed to adjust the consistency of the chili to your liking. Check the seasoning, adding salt and pepper to taste. Serve topped with tortilla chips and some cilantro leaves.

This chili can be refrigerated in an airtight container for up to 6 days or frozen for up to 6 months.

Vegan Carrot, Yam, and Ginger Soup

∘ MAKES 6 CUPS (4 PORTIONS) ∘

Okay, we know, there are hundreds if not thousands of recipes for carrot ginger soup. And there's good reason for that: it's so damn delicious. Ours is subtly yet proudly different with hints of lime and cinnamon, and made smooth by coconut milk instead of cream or milk (yes, it's vegan!), and topped with one of our favorite garnishes, cilantro. When this soup hits our menu in the winter, there's barely enough to feed the masses, and our staff have been known to pre-order quarts of it to take home (because they know how tasty it is and how quickly we run out).

INGREDIENTS

- 3 tablespoons coconut oil
- 1½ cups diced onion
- 2 cloves garlic, minced
- 2 tablespoons minced ginger
- ¼ teaspoon ground cinnamon
- 1 teaspoon sweet paprika
- Salt and freshly ground black pepper
- 3 cups diced-small carrots
- 1½ cups diced sweet potato
- 2 cups low-sodium vegetable broth
- ½ cup coconut milk
- 2 tablespoons lime juice
- Cilantro leaves, for garnish

DIRECTIONS

In a Dutch oven, warm the coconut oil over medium-low heat. Add the onion, garlic, and ginger and cook, stirring occasionally, until the onion softens and becomes translucent, about 5 minutes. Stir in the cinnamon and paprika and season lightly with salt and pepper. Continue to cook until the spices are fragrant, about 2 minutes.

Add the carrots, sweet potato, and broth. Bring to a boil, then lower the heat and simmer, covered, until the carrots and sweet potato are tender, 25 to 30 minutes.

Stir in the coconut milk and lime juice. Puree the soup in a blender (or directly in the pot using an immersion blender) until smooth. Check the seasoning, adjusting with salt and pepper to taste. Serve topped with the cilantro leaves.

This soup can be refrigerated in an airtight container for up to 7 days or frozen for up to 6 months.

Creamy Mushroom Soup

· MAKES 6 CUPS (4 PORTIONS) ·

All hail the almighty mushroom—or in this case mushroom soup! There's something undeniably scrumptious about sautéed mushrooms, and there are so many different kinds. This soup is silky, smooth, filling, earthy, savory, and aromatic . . . and you will not have any leftovers, trust us.

A vegan alternative for this soup is possible by omitting the cream, but the cream definitely gives a "next level" depth and satisfying layer to it. If you're looking for even more dairy fattiness (if you're into it, you know what we're talking about), sauté the mushrooms in both olive oil and butter (the olive oil will help keep the butter from burning). You can also swap out the veggie broth for chicken if that's all you have on hand.

INGREDIENTS

- ¼ cup olive oil
- 1 medium onion, diced small
- 2 cloves garlic, minced
- 1 stalk celery, diced small
- 1 teaspoon thyme leaves
- Salt and freshly ground black pepper
- 1 portobello mushroom, stalk and gills removed, coarsely chopped
- 1 pound cremini and/or button mushrooms, sliced thin
- ¼ cup minced flat-leaf parsley, + extra for garnish
- 4 cups low-sodium vegetable broth
- ½ cup heavy cream
- Maldon salt flakes

DIRECTIONS

In a Dutch oven, warm 3 tablespoons of the olive oil over medium-low heat. Add the onion, garlic, celery, and thyme and cook, stirring occasionally, until the onions begin to soften, 3 to 4 minutes. Season lightly with salt and pepper.

Increase the heat to medium and stir in the portobello mushroom, half of the cremini mushrooms, and 3 tablespoons of the parsley. Cook until the mushrooms have released all their water and started to brown nicely around their edges, stirring very occasionally, about 10 minutes.

Add the vegetable broth to the pot, bring to a boil, lower the heat, and simmer until the mushrooms are completely tender, about 10 minutes.

While the soup is simmering, heat the remaining 1 tablespoon of olive oil a large sauté pan over high heat, and stir in the remaining cremini mushrooms and parsley. Sauté until the mushrooms have released all their water and browned well, about 7 minutes. Remove from the heat.

Puree the soup in a blender (or directly in the pot using an immersion blender) until smooth. Check the seasoning and adjust with salt and pepper to taste. Stir in the cream. Serve topped with the sautéed mushroom slices, a sprinkle of minced parsley, and some Maldon salt flakes.

This soup can be refrigerated in an airtight container for up to 6 days or frozen for up to 6 months.

Leek and Pear Soup

◦ MAKES 6 CUPS (4 PORTIONS) ◦

We love the delicate flavors of both leeks and pears; they're often the overlooked relatives of onions and apples. Combining them in this silky pureed soup created a delightful surprise to our taste buds and our customers' palates. We love stirring some heavy cooking cream in at the end, but you can keep it vegan by using a coconut cream instead, or a mellow-flavored dairy-free milk such as oat, almond, or rice (just make sure it's unsweetened). A lovely, high-end garnish option for this soup is a little hazelnut oil drizzled on top, with a sprinkling of fresh thyme leaves.

INGREDIENTS

- 2 tablespoons olive oil
- 1 medium onion, diced small
- 1 leek, white and pale green parts only, sliced thin
- 1 russet potato, cubed small
- 1 celery stalk, sliced thin
- 2 teaspoons picked thyme leaves
- 1 bay leaf
- Salt and freshly ground black pepper
- 4 pears, peeled, cored and quartered
- 3 cups low-sodium vegetable broth
- ½ cup heavy cream (optional)
- 1 teaspoon hazelnut oil

DIRECTIONS

In a Dutch oven, warm the olive oil over medium-low heat. Add the onion, leek, potato, and celery and cook, stirring occasionally, until the onion and leek soften, about 5 minutes. Stir in 1 teaspoon of the thyme and the bay leaf and season lightly with salt and pepper. Continue to cook until the spices are fragrant, about 2 minutes.

Add the pears and broth. Bring to a boil, then lower the heat and simmer, covered, until the potatoes are very tender, 20 to 25 minutes. Remove and discard the bay leaf.

Puree the soup in a blender (or directly in the pot using an immersion blender) until smooth. Check the seasoning and adjust with salt and pepper to taste. Stir in the cream. Serve topped with hazelnut oil and the remaining thyme leaves.

This soup can be refrigerated in an airtight container for up to 7 days or frozen for up to 6 months.

Pumpkin Spice Soup

∘ MAKES 6 CUPS (4 PORTIONS) ∘

This soup just tastes like fall: Halloween, cozy cable-knit sweaters, and pumpkin carving. It's one of our absolute favorites, as well as one of our customers' most cherished seasonal soups. We love a splash of cream at the end, but vegans can celebrate, as it's just as tasty without! Instead, try adding a few toasted pecans for some crunch and extra autumn flair.

INGREDIENTS

- 3 tablespoons olive oil
- 2 cups diced onion
- 4 cups diced butternut squash
- 4 cups diced sweet potato
- 1 cup diced carrot
- ½ teaspoon ground cinnamon
- ⅛ teaspoon ground nutmeg
- ⅛ teaspoon ground clove
- Salt and freshly ground black pepper
- 4 cups low-sodium vegetable broth
- ½ cup heavy cream
- Thyme leaves, for garnish

DIRECTIONS

In a Dutch oven, warm the olive oil over medium-low heat. Add the onion, squash, sweet potato, and carrots and cook, stirring occasionally, until the onions soften and become translucent, about 5 minutes. Stir in the cinnamon, nutmeg, and clove and season lightly with salt and pepper. Continue to cook until the spices are fragrant, about 2 minutes.

Add the broth. Bring to a boil, then lower the heat and simmer, covered, until the vegetables are tender, 25 to 30 minutes.

Puree the soup in a blender (or directly in the pot using an immersion blender) until smooth. Check the seasoning and adjust with salt and pepper to taste. Stir in the cream. Serve topped with a sprinkling of thyme leaves.

This soup can be refrigerated in an airtight container for up to 7 days or frozen for up to 6 months.

Mandy's Ribollita

∘ MAKES 6 CUPS (4 PORTIONS) ∘

Ribollita is a classic Tuscan bean soup. Our take is sans bread, although a delicious baguette on the side for dipping never hurt anyone. Like many of our salads, this soup is a feast for the eyes, with so many colored veggies like carrots, tomatoes, lacinato kale, and tons of fresh herbs. You will not be hungry after this soup.

INGREDIENTS

- 3 tablespoons olive oil
- 1 small onion, diced small
- 3 cloves garlic, minced
- 1 bay leaf
- 1 tablespoon minced sage
- 1 tablespoon minced rosemary
- Salt and freshly ground black pepper
- 1 small carrot, sliced lengthwise and cut into half-moons
- 1 small zucchini, sliced lengthwise and cut into half-moons
- 1 14-ounce (398 ml) can whole peeled tomatoes
- 3 cups low-sodium vegetable broth
- 1 14-ounce (398 ml) can cannellini or borlotti beans, drained and rinsed
- 1 bunch lacinato kale, stems removed, cut into ribbons
- ¼ cup grated Parmesan
- Basil leaves, for garnish

DIRECTIONS

In a Dutch oven, warm the olive oil over medium-low heat. Add the onion, garlic, bay leaf, sage, and rosemary and cook, stirring occasionally, until the onion begins to soften, about 5 minutes. Season lightly with salt and pepper.

Add the carrot, zucchini, canned tomatoes, and broth to the pot, using a wooden spoon or spatula to break up the tomatoes to release their juices.

Bring to a boil, lower the heat, and simmer until the carrots are completely tender, 25 to 30 minutes.

Remove and discard the bay leaf. Stir in the beans, kale, and cheese. Cook for a further 2 minutes, until the kale wilts. Check the seasoning and adjust with salt and pepper to taste. Serve topped with the basil leaves.

This soup can be refrigerated in an airtight container for up to 7 days or frozen for up to 6 months.

Roasted Garlic and Butternut Squash Soup

◦ MAKES 6 CUPS (4 PORTIONS) ◦

This is a very simple recipe, and the inspiration behind it, like most of our recipes, stems from a happy childhood memory. Every year, our family would travel to Florida for March break—in classic Montreal snowbird style—and on the way, we always stopped at Prezzo, an Italian restaurant on the outskirts of Boca Raton. Instead of a typical olive oil to dip our warm crusty bread into, Prezzo would serve whole heads of squishy caramelized garlic, and we would delight in smearing the cloves straight onto the bread. We devoured more garlic than should be possible, so how we made it to the appetizers or mains is anyone's guess. For this recipe, we took the memory of roasted garlic, added some seasonal gourds, and blended it all up into a satisfying winter soup.

INGREDIENTS

- 1 whole head garlic, divided into cloves and peeled
- 2 small butternut squashes, cut into 1-inch cubes (about 8 cups)
- ¼ cup olive oil
- Salt and freshly ground black pepper
- 1 cup diced-small onion
- 2 teaspoons thyme leaves
- 3 cups low-sodium vegetable broth

DIRECTIONS

Preheat the oven to 375°F.

In a large bowl, toss the garlic and squash with 3 tablespoons of the olive oil and a generous amount of salt and pepper. Transfer and spread out on a 13-by-9-inch sheet tray and roast in the oven until the squash is very soft, 40 to 45 minutes.

In a Dutch oven, heat the remaining 1 tablespoon of olive oil over medium-low heat. Add the onion and 1 teaspoon of the thyme and cook, stirring occasionally, until the onion softens and becomes translucent, about 5 minutes.

Add the roasted squash and garlic to the pot, followed by the vegetable broth. Bring to a boil, then lower the heat and simmer for a few minutes.

Puree the soup in a blender (or directly in the pot using an immersion blender) until smooth. Check the seasoning, and adjust with salt and pepper to taste. Serve topped with the remaining thyme leaves.

This soup can be refrigerated in an airtight container for up to 6 to 7 days or frozen for up to 6 months.

Curried Sweet Potato and Cauliflower Soup

◦ MAKES 6 CUPS (4 PORTIONS) ◦

When this soup is on the stovetop, the powerful, intoxicating smell of curry permeates the entire restaurant, making our staff excited first and then pretty much guaranteeing that any hungry customer coming in orders this for their meal. Home cooks, crank your oven fans for this one! And vegans rejoice, this one is for you too.

INGREDIENTS

- 2 cups 1-inch cubed sweet potato
- ½ head cauliflower, cut into florets (about 6 cups)
- ½ cup ½-inch cubed carrot
- 1 small onion, cut into ½-inch cubes
- 3 tablespoons olive oil
- 1 tablespoon garam masala
- 2 teaspoons ground cumin
- 1 teaspoon salt
- ½ teaspoon freshly ground black pepper
- 3 cups low-sodium vegetable broth
- Cilantro leaves, for garnish

DIRECTIONS

Preheat the oven to 375°F.

In a large bowl, toss the sweet potato, cauliflower, carrots, and onion with the olive oil, garam masala, cumin, salt, and pepper. Spread out onto a 13-by-9-inch sheet tray and roast in the oven until the vegetables are very soft, 45 to 50 minutes.

Transfer to a Dutch oven and pour in the vegetable broth. Bring to a boil, then lower the heat and simmer for a few minutes to combine the flavors.

Puree the soup in a blender (or directly in the pot using an immersion blender) until smooth. Check the seasoning and adjust with salt and pepper to taste. Serve topped with cilantro.

This soup can be refrigerated in an airtight container for up to 7 days or frozen for up to 6 months.

Veggie, Fennel, and Barley Soup

◦ MAKES 6 CUPS (4 PORTIONS) ◦

We have always made a point of asking our staff to send us their favorite recipes or cooking inspirations, and we even set up a designated email address for our staff to send us their input on our recipes. We review the account daily, and often it's full of golden recipe nuggets. One of our key staff members, Kelsey Hops, is obsessed with this soup. Every fall she asks us when we'll start making it, and every year she is our key taste tester to make sure its taste profile and stellar quality are just as good as she remembers it from the year before.

A fun or flexible option with this soup is that you can swap out the barley for farro (and remember to make extra so you have a cooked grain ready in your fridge to bulk up a salad or make a comforting grain bowl). Oh, but please don't omit the fennel; it adds a layer of flavor that's unmatched. You can make a vegan version of this soup simply by omitting the Parmesan.

INGREDIENTS

- 3 tablespoons olive oil
- 1 cup diced-small fennel
- 1 cup diced-small onion
- 2 cloves garlic, minced
- Salt and freshly ground black pepper
- 1 14-ounce (398 ml) can diced tomatoes
- 1 14-ounce (398 ml) can navy beans, drained and rinsed
- 3 cups low-sodium vegetable broth
- 1 cup cooked pot barley (or farro)
- 2 cups packed baby spinach
- ¼ cup grated Parmesan
- ¼ cup coarsely chopped basil
- Basil leaves, for garnish

DIRECTIONS

In a Dutch oven, warm the olive oil over medium-low heat. Add the fennel, onion, and garlic and cook, stirring occasionally, until the fennel and onion soften and become translucent, about 5 minutes. Season lightly with salt and pepper.

Add the canned tomatoes, beans, and broth to the pot and bring to a boil. Reduce the heat to low and simmer for 5 minutes.

Stir in the barley, spinach, Parmesan, and chopped basil, and continue to simmer until the spinach has wilted, about 2 minutes. Check the seasoning and adjust with salt and pepper to taste. Serve topped with the basil leaves.

This soup can be refrigerated in an airtight container for up to 7 days or frozen for up to 6 months.

Peanut Butter, Lentil, and Chickpea Soup

◦ MAKES 6 CUPS (4 PORTIONS) ◦

MANDY | OK, hands down, this is my favorite soup. Yes, I love anything peanut butter or peanuts (sorry to anyone with a peanut allergy!). This combination of ingredients may seem unlikely, but trust me, it's an absolute winner. The PB gives it a creaminess that's satiating, the legumes add some veggie protein and heartiness, and everything else in here is pure explosive flavor and gorgeous color.

INGREDIENTS

- 3 tablespoons olive oil
- ¾ cup diced onion
- ½ cup diced red bell pepper
- 1 garlic clove, minced
- 1 teaspoon ground cumin
- ½ teaspoon Sriracha sauce
- Salt and freshly ground black pepper
- 1 14-ounce (398 ml) can diced tomatoes
- 1 cup cooked green lentils
- ½ cup canned chickpeas, drained and rinsed
- 3 cups low-sodium vegetable broth
- ½ cup cooked brown rice
- ¼ cup + 1 tablespoon creamy peanut butter
- ¼ cup minced cilantro
- ¼ cup roasted peanuts, for garnish
- Cilantro leaves, for garnish

DIRECTIONS

In a Dutch oven, warm the olive oil over medium-low heat. Add the onion, red pepper, and garlic and cook, stirring occasionally, until the vegetables start to soften, about 5 minutes. Stir in the cumin and Sriracha and season lightly with salt and pepper.

Add the canned tomatoes, lentils, chickpeas, and broth to the pot and bring to a boil. Reduce the heat to low and simmer for 5 to 10 minutes to combine the flavors.

Stir in the rice, followed by the peanut butter and cilantro, and simmer a further 2 minutes. Adjust seasoning to taste with salt and pepper. You may wish to add a dash more Sriracha to taste. Serve topped with 1 tablespoon of roasted peanuts per bowl and some cilantro leaves.

This soup can be refrigerated in an airtight container for up to 5 days or frozen for up to 6 months.

Curried Lentil Soup

◦ MAKES 6 CUPS (4 PORTIONS) ◦

The many Indian restaurants up on Rue Jean-Talon and Boulevard de l'Acadie in Montreal are brimming with the most delectable goodies, stews, and soups. For this soup, we tried to combine some of our favorite inspirations from places like Bombay Mahal Express, Pushap, Atma, Chand Palace, Malhi Sweets, and Le 409. Some people may have had lackluster experiences with lentil soup before, but this one has so many vibrant pops of flavor—between the ginger, spicy cayenne, lime juice, and tomatoes—it'll brighten your palate on the dreariest of days. And it's vegan to boot.

INGREDIENTS

- 3 tablespoons coconut oil
- 1 medium onion, diced small
- 2 cloves garlic, minced
- 3 tablespoons minced ginger
- 1 tablespoon ground cumin
- ⅛ teaspoon cayenne
- Salt and freshly ground black pepper
- 1½ cups uncooked green lentils
- 4 cups low-sodium vegetable broth
- 1 14-ounce (398 ml) can crushed tomatoes
- 1 tablespoon maple syrup
- 1 tablespoon lime juice
- Cilantro, for garnish

DIRECTIONS

In a Dutch oven, warm the coconut oil over medium-low heat. Add the onion, garlic, and ginger and cook, stirring occasionally, until the onion softens and becomes translucent, about 5 minutes. Stir in the cumin and cayenne and season lightly with salt and pepper. Continue to cook until the spices are fragrant, about 2 minutes. Add the lentils and broth. Bring to a boil, then lower the heat and simmer, covered, until the lentils are tender but not mushy, 25 to 30 minutes.

Stir in the crushed tomatoes, maple syrup, and lime juice. Check the seasoning and adjust with salt, pepper, and more lime juice. Serve with cilantro to garnish.

This soup can be refrigerated in an airtight container for up to 7 days or frozen for up to 6 months.

Easy Tom Kha Soup

◦ MAKES 6 CUPS (4 PORTIONS) ◦

MANDY | I spent 6 months crisscrossing Thailand, Vietnam, Laos, and Cambodia, where I fell in love with the people, their customs, their kindness, and more than anything, their food. At the time, I was a strict vegan! When I was staying in villages where no English was spoken, I would draw pictures of animals on a paper napkin with a large X over top to indicate that I didn't eat meat or fish. Locals would laugh and then point to something on their menu, nodding their understanding. Then they would bring me some of the most delectable meals I have ever had. One of those was a tom kha soup made with vegetables (rather than the more commonly found tom kha gai, with chicken). I've adapted that to create the soup here.

NOTE: IF YOU WANT TO MAKE THIS SOUP VEGAN, OMIT THE FISH SAUCE.

INGREDIENTS

- 3 tablespoons coconut oil
- 1 cup small-diced red onion
- 1 cup small-diced red bell pepper
- 1 cup small-diced Japanese eggplant
- ½ cup thinly shredded red cabbage
- 2 garlic cloves, minced
- 2 tablespoons minced ginger
- 1 Thai chili, finely chopped
- 1 tablespoon coconut sugar (or brown or cane sugar)
- Salt
- 2 cups low-sodium vegetable broth or water
- 1 14-ounce (398 ml) can coconut milk
- 2 cups cubed firm tofu
- 1 cup cut-small broccoli florets
- 2 tablespoons fish sauce (optional)
- 1 tablespoon tamari or soy sauce
- 2 tablespoons lime juice
- ¼ cup coarsely chopped cilantro
- ¼ cup thinly sliced scallions
- Cilantro leaves, for garnish

DIRECTIONS

In a Dutch oven, warm the coconut oil over medium-low heat. Add the onion, red pepper, eggplant, red cabbage, garlic, ginger, and chili and cook, stirring occasionally, until the vegetables soften, 5 to 7 minutes. Stir in the sugar and season lightly with salt. Add the broth and coconut milk. Bring to a boil, then lower the heat and simmer for 5 minutes. Stir in the tofu and broccoli florets and continue to cook for another 5 minutes.

Remove from the heat and stir in the fish sauce, tamari, lime juice, and cilantro. Check the seasoning and adjust with salt and pepper. Serve topped with sliced scallions and cilantro leaves.

This soup can be refrigerated in an airtight container for up to 7 days or frozen for up to 6 months.

Black Bean Soup

∘ MAKES 6 CUPS (4 PORTIONS) ∘

After our foray into soups-we-could-make-with-ingredients-we-had-on-hand-in-our-restaurants, one of our veteran kitchen goddesses, Alyssa MacEwan, came to us with a modified recipe from one of our favorite plant-based cookbooks: *The Moosewood Cookbook*. The recipe she shared was for a hearty black bean puree that was spicy and unusually flavored with a splash of freshly squeezed orange juice. We wanted to Mandy-ize it, so we added fresh lime juice and zest, and customers could order it with an extra topping of diced creamy avocado. For a hearty dinner option, we suggest adding strips of Seared Filet Mignon (page 120).

INGREDIENTS

- 3 tablespoons olive oil
- 2 cups small-diced onion
- 1 cup small-diced carrot
- 1 cup small-diced red bell pepper
- 2 cloves garlic, minced
- 2 teaspoons ground cumin
- ⅛ teaspoon cayenne
- Salt and freshly ground black pepper
- 3 14-ounce (398 ml) cans black beans, drained and rinsed
- 3 cups low-sodium vegetable broth
- ⅓ cup orange juice
- Zest and juice of 1 lime
- Cilantro leaves, for garnish

DIRECTIONS

In a Dutch oven, warm the olive oil over medium-low heat. Add the onion, carrot, ½ cup of the red pepper, and the garlic and cook, stirring occasionally, until the onions soften and become translucent, about 5 minutes. Stir in the cumin and cayenne and season lightly with salt and pepper. Continue to cook until the spices are fragrant.

Add 3 cups of the black beans to the pot, reserving the rest for garnish. Add the vegetable broth, bring to a boil, and reduce the heat to low, simmering the mixture until the carrots are very soft, 20 to 25 minutes.

Stir in the orange juice, lime juice and zest, and season to taste with salt and pepper. Puree the soup in a blender (or directly in the pot using an immersion blender) until you reach desired consistency (at Mandy's, we don't like to puree TOO much, as we still want a bit of the texture and feel of the black beans).

Check the seasoning and adjust with salt and pepper. Garnish each bowl of soup with 1 tablespoon of the reserved black beans, 2 tablespoons diced red pepper, and the cilantro leaves.

This soup can be refrigerated in an airtight container for up to 6 days or frozen for up to 6 months.

Lohikeitto (Finnish Salmon Soup)

◦ MAKES 6 CUPS (4 PORTIONS) ◦

MANDY | One dreary February, our dear friend Belle Bourduas (the namesake of our Belle Salad) was headed to Finland for work, and mentioned she would be stopping over in Stockholm, Sweden, for a weekend on her way home. We sighed with wanderlust . . . We had accumulated a ridiculous number of travel points, hadn't taken a break from work or kids in YEARS, and had always been obsessed with Scandinavia's design, progressive politics, strange foods, and love of all things winter. So, on a lark, Becca and I booked ourselves flights and joined Belle for a whirlwind jet-lagged but eye-opening weekend. We fell in love with a most scrumptious Finnish soup that celebrates the abundance of Atlantic salmon in the North Sea and the Baltic Sea: lohikeitto (pronounced "lo-hee-kay-toe"). When we got back to our side of the Atlantic, we had to recreate it, with a few tweaks! If you're put off by the thought that it might be too fishy, we promise you, this is an astonishing way to cook salmon that yields a mild, comforting soup. Even the children in your life will love it. You'll find yourself making it way more often than you might expect!

INGREDIENTS

- 3 tablespoons unsalted butter
- 2 cups sliced leek, white parts only
- 1¼ cups small-diced russet potato
- 1 cup chopped carrot
- ¼ teaspoon ground nutmeg
- Salt and freshly ground black pepper
- 3 cups low-sodium chicken broth
- 10 ounces Atlantic salmon, skin removed, cut into 1½-inch cubes
- ¾ cup corn kernels
- ½ cup heavy cream
- 1 to 2 tablespoons lemon juice
- ¼ cup minced dill
- Chopped dill, for garnish

DIRECTIONS

In a Dutch oven, melt the butter over medium-low heat. Add the leek, cover, and sweat until softened, stirring occasionally, about 5 minutes.

Stir in the potato and carrot and continue to cook for another 5 minutes.

Stir in the nutmeg and season lightly with salt and pepper. Continue to cook until the spices are fragrant, another minute or so.

Pour in the broth. Bring to a gentle boil, then lower the heat and simmer until the potatoes are just tender, about 10 minutes. Add the cubed salmon and corn, and simmer for another 5 minutes until the fish is poached through.

Stir in the cream, lemon juice, and dill. Check the seasoning and adjust with additional lemon juice, salt, and pepper as needed. Serve topped with the dill.

This soup can be refrigerated in an airtight container for up to 4 days or frozen for up to 3 months.

The Bubby Soup

In Yiddish, bubby means "grandmother," and this recipe is our bubby's (aka: Granny Bernice's) recipe. Like any good bubby, she would make enough of this soup to feed the entire island of Montreal. It's a life-affirming elixir, really, packed full of vegetal flavor. And while this soup is traditionally eaten at Passover, it can be enjoyed all year round, and is our favorite comfort food on colder days.

NOTE: THIS SOUP DEPENDS ON ITS DELICIOUS HOMEMADE CHICKEN STOCK, WHICH SIMMERS FOR AT LEAST 3 HOURS (AND UP TO 6), AND NEEDS TO COOL OVERNIGHT. THE MATZO BALLS FOR THE SOUP NEED TO CHILL FOR AT LEAST 1 HOUR. PLAN ACCORDINGLY. THE SOUP CAN BE MADE 2 OR 3 DAYS AHEAD AND KEPT REFRIGERATED; THE MATZO MEAL MIXTURE CAN BE MADE A DAY AHEAD AND CHILLED.

INGREDIENTS

STOCK

- 1 3-to-4-pound whole chicken
- 3 cups coarsely chopped onion
- 3 cups coarsely chopped carrots
- 3 cups coarsely chopped (with leafy tops) celery
- 2 bay leaves
- 1 bunch parsley stems
- ¼ teaspoon celery seed
- 20 whole black peppercorns

DIRECTIONS

Make the stock
In a large stockpot over medium-high heat, combine the whole chicken, onion, carrots, celery, bay leaves, parsley stems, celery seed, and peppercorns and add enough water (3.5 to 4 quarts) to cover the contents of the pot. Bring to a gentle boil, lower the heat to medium-low, and simmer for 20 minutes, skimming scum from the top.

Cover and simmer the stock for 1 hour, then lift the chicken out of the cooking liquid. Set it on a tray or large plate, and using a sharp knife, and tongs to secure the chicken, remove the breasts and transfer them to a plate. Return the remaining chicken to the pot for a minimum of 2 hours, and up to 5 hours, simmering (the longer you leave it, the deeper the chicken flavor will be). Shred the removed chicken breast, transfer to a container, and splash with a little of the stock. Let cool, then cover and refrigerate.

After the additional 2 to 5 hours simmering, remove the stock from the heat and allow it to cool overnight, either in the fridge or, if the temperature is close to freezing outside, tightly covered on a balcony or patio.

SOUP

- Salt and freshly ground black pepper
- ½ cup shredded carrot
- ¼ cup thinly sliced celery
- ¼ cup minced dill
- 2 tablespoons thinly sliced scallions
- 1 recipe Matzo Balls (see below)
- Dill fronds, for garnish

The next day, strain the stock through a fine-mesh sieve into a Dutch oven or large saucepan (or an airtight container if you're not using it immediately). Discard the strained solids; you should have approximately 3 quarts of stock. If the stock has set due to a high collagen content, you may have to warm it up slightly to return it to its liquid state.

Assemble the soup

In a Dutch oven or large saucepan, warm about 1 quart of the stock, seasoning it well with salt and pepper. Add the carrot and celery, bring the liquid to a boil, and add the reserved shredded chicken breast. Simmer for 10 to 15 minutes, until the vegetables are tender. Stir in the minced dill and scallions. Cover and keep warm over very low heat.

Meanwhile, in a large saucepan, bring the remaining 2 quarts of your chicken stock to a boil and season to taste with salt and pepper. Gently lower the matzo balls into the pot of well-seasoned stock and simmer gently for 15 minutes or so, until the balls are cooked through.

Use a slotted spoon to transfer 3 warm matzo balls into each serving bowl. Ladle warm soup over the balls and top with fresh strands of dill (enough to make Bubby proud) and some freshly ground pepper.

This soup can be refrigerated in an airtight container for up to 5 days or frozen for up to 3 months.

MATZO BALLS

MAKES 12 MATZO BALLS

INGREDIENTS

- 1 cup matzo meal (or about 4½ ounces/125 g finely ground matzos)
- 3 large eggs, whisked
- ¼ cup olive or sunflower oil
- ¼ cup sparkling water
- ½ teaspoon Kosher salt
- 1 teaspoon chicken bouillon powder (preferably kosher, such as Osem Chicken Style Consomme Soup and Seasoning Mix)

NOTE: YOU CAN PURCHASE CLASSIC MATZO BALL MIXES LIKE STREIT'S, MANISCHEWITZ, OR YEHUDA MATZOS, OR MAKE YOUR OWN (AS WE DO HERE) BY TURNING MATZOS INTO MATZO MEAL IN A FOOD PROCESSOR OR A BLENDER AND SEASONING THE MEAL WITH SALT AND CHICKEN BOUILLON POWDER.

DIRECTIONS

In a bowl, use a fork to combine the matzo meal, eggs, oil, sparkling water, salt, and bouillon powder until the mixture looks like wet sand (don't worry, it firms up as it chills). Cover and refrigerate for 1 hour or more.

Using a tablespoon and working with wet hands (we like to keep a bowl of warm water next to us to dip our fingers into), scoop out 2 tablespoons of matzo mixture (about 33 g, if you're using a scale) and lightly shape into a ball. Set aside on a plate or small tray and repeat with the rest of the mixture. You should have 12 balls in total.

Potato, Leek, and Parmesan Soup

◦ MAKES 6 CUPS (4 PORTIONS) ◦

Yeah, yeah, you've heard and seen all the potato leek soups before . . .
or have you? Ours is a customer and staff fave, with the rosemary
popping up as an unexpected, underlying highlight, and salty Parmesan
giving it a final kick. This soup is a sure crowd-pleaser.

INGREDIENTS

- 3 tablespoons unsalted butter
- 5 cups thinly sliced leeks (white and pale green parts only)
- 2 cups diced-small russet potatoes
- 1 rosemary sprig
- Salt and freshly ground black pepper
- 3 cups low-sodium vegetable broth
- ¼ cup grated Parmesan
- 4 whole basil leaves, for garnish
- 1 tablespoon fresh Parmesan shavings, for garnish

DIRECTIONS

In a Dutch oven, warm the butter over medium-low heat. Add the leeks and cook, covered but stirring occasionally, until the leeks soften, about 5 minutes. Stir in the potatoes and rosemary and season lightly with salt and pepper. Continue to cook until fragrant, about 2 minutes.

Add the broth. Bring to a boil, then lower the heat and simmer, covered, until the potatoes are very tender, 20 to 25 minutes. Remove and discard the rosemary stem.

Puree the soup in a blender (or directly in the pot using an immersion blender) until smooth. Check the seasoning and adjust with salt and pepper to taste. Stir in the grated Parmesan. Serve topped with the basil leaves and Parmesan shavings.

This soup can be refrigerated in an airtight container for up to 7 days or frozen for up to 6 months.

Smoky Cumin Southern Chicken Soup

◦ MAKES 6 CUPS (4 PORTIONS) ◦

After our veggie quinoa chili became so popular, we started getting requests from guests asking if we offered a similar soup, but with more protein, aka chicken (chicken is our biggest-selling add-on to any soup or salad—well, biggest-selling after our cookies, but that's a whole other story). What's great about this soup, other than its delicious smoky and slightly spicy flavor, is that you probably have all of these ingredients in your pantry. Don't feel like cooking chicken breasts? Pick up a rotisserie chicken at your local grocery store and shred the breasts (save the rest for another soup or salad add-on). Provecho!

INGREDIENTS

- 2 medium (7-ounce) skinless boneless chicken breasts
- 2 teaspoons Montreal steak spice (see note on page 195)
- ¼ cup olive oil
- 1 small onion, diced small
- 2 cloves garlic, minced
- ½ teaspoon cayenne
- ½ teaspoon ground cumin
- ½ teaspoon pimentòn (aka Spanish smoked paprika)
- ¼ teaspoon red pepper flakes
- Salt and freshly ground black pepper
- 1 red bell pepper, sliced into thin strips
- 1 14-ounce (398 ml) can diced tomatoes
- 2 cups low-sodium chicken broth
- ½ cup corn kernels
- ½ cup black beans
- Cilantro leaves, for garnish

DIRECTIONS

Preheat the oven to 350°F.

In a bowl, combine the chicken, Montreal steak spice, and 2 tablespoons of the olive oil, and mix well to coat.

Transfer to a parchment-lined sheet tray and bake for 30 minutes, until cooked through. Allow to cool slightly before using a fork to shred the chicken into thin pieces. Set aside.

In a Dutch oven, warm the remaining 2 tablespoons of olive oil over medium-low heat. Add the onion and garlic and cook, stirring occasionally, until the onion softens, about 5 minutes. Stir in the cayenne, cumin, pimentòn, and red pepper flakes. Season lightly with salt and pepper.

Add the red pepper strips, the canned tomatoes, and the chicken broth. Bring to a boil, then lower the heat and simmer for 7 to 10 minutes.

Stir in the shredded chicken, corn, and black beans. Check the seasoning and adjust with salt and pepper to taste. Serve topped with cilantro leaves.

This soup can be refrigerated in an airtight container for up to 5 days or frozen for up to 3 months.

Chicken Soup with Lemon and Orzo

◦ MAKES 6 CUPS (4 PORTIONS) ◦

This soup is a fresher, zestier, lighter spin on a traditional chicken noodle soup. We adore the flash of lemon from the zest, the peppery seasoning of the chicken, and how it all comes together perfectly for a hopeful hint of spring after a long Montreal winter.

NOTE: IF YOU DON'T HAVE MONTREAL STEAK SPICE, YOU CAN MAKE YOUR OWN BLEND BY COMBINING 1 TEASPOON BLACK PEPPER, 1 TEASPOON SWEET PAPRIKA, 1 TEASPOON SALT, ½ TEASPOON GARLIC POWDER, ½ TEASPOON ONION POWDER, ⅛ TEASPOON CAYENNE, ½ TEASPOON GROUND CORIANDER, AND ½ TEASPOON DILL SEED. THIS BLEND WILL KEEP IN A SMALL AIRTIGHT JAR FOR A LONG TIME.

INGREDIENTS

- 2 medium (7-ounce) skinless boneless chicken breasts
- 2 teaspoons Montreal steak spice (see note)
- ¼ cup olive oil
- 1 leek, pale green and white parts only, sliced thin
- 2 stalks celery, sliced thin
- Salt and freshly ground black pepper
- 4 cups low-sodium chicken broth
- 1 cup cooked orzo
- ¼ cup minced dill
- ¼ cup lemon juice
- Dill fronds, for garnish

DIRECTIONS

Preheat the oven to 350°F.

In a bowl, combine the chicken, Montreal steak spice, and 2 tablespoons of the olive oil. Mix well to coat.

Transfer the chicken to a parchment-lined sheet tray. Bake for 30 minutes or until cooked through. Allow to cool slightly before using a fork to shred the chicken into thin pieces. Set aside.

In a Dutch oven, warm the remaining 2 tablespoons of olive oil over medium-low heat. Add the leek and celery and cook, stirring occasionally, until the vegetables soften, about 5 minutes. Season lightly with salt and pepper.

Add the chicken broth. Bring to a boil, then lower the heat and simmer for 7 to 10 minutes.

Stir in the shredded chicken and cooked orzo and season with salt and pepper. Stir in the minced dill and lemon juice and check the seasoning once more, adjusting as needed with lemon juice, dill, salt, and more freshly ground pepper.

This soup can be refrigerated in an airtight container for up to 5 days or frozen for up to 4 months.

Chicken and Pearl Couscous Soup

∘ MAKES 6 CUPS (4 PORTIONS) ∘

When you live in Montreal, where it's winter half the year, you find yourself reaching for a basic chicken noodle soup or chicken elixir weekly. In our kitchens, we are always looking for ways to put a spin on the classics; here we swapped out the noodles for pearl couscous and added more ginger and turmeric for some extra anti-cold, anti-inflammatory properties.

INGREDIENTS

- 3 tablespoons olive oil
- 1 small onion, diced small
- 3 garlic cloves, minced
- 1 stalk celery, sliced thin
- 1 cup diced-small carrots
- 1 teaspoon minced ginger
- ½ teaspoon ground turmeric
- 1 teaspoon thyme leaves
- Salt and freshly ground black pepper
- 1 large (10-ounce) skinless boneless chicken breast
- 4 cups low-sodium chicken broth
- ½ cup uncooked pearl couscous

DIRECTIONS

In a Dutch oven, warm the olive oil over medium-low heat. Add the onion, garlic, celery, and carrots and cook, stirring occasionally, until the vegetables start to soften, about 5 minutes.

Stir in the ginger, turmeric, and thyme, and season lightly with salt and pepper. Cook for another 2 minutes until the spices are fragrant.

Add the chicken breast and broth. Bring to a boil, then lower the heat and simmer for 25 to 30 minutes.

In a medium saucepan, bring 4 cups of water to a boil. Salt the water heavily and cook the pearl couscous until al dente, 6 to 8 minutes. Strain and set aside.

Remove the chicken breast from the pot. Allow to cool slightly before using a fork to shred the chicken into thin pieces. Return the chicken to the pot and continue to simmer until the carrots are completely tender. Stir in the cooked pearl couscous. Check the seasoning, adjusting with salt and pepper to taste. Serve.

This soup can be refrigerated in an airtight container for up to 5 days or frozen for up to 4 months.

Sweets

★ CHAPTER FIVE ★

Blueberry Citrus Cake

◦ MAKES ONE 9-INCH LOAF OR 9-INCH SQUARE CAKE (SERVES 8) ◦

This cake is a mix between traditional coffee cake and blueberry buckle, complete with a streusel topping made by blending some butter and flour into the sugar and cinnamon. It's a winter staple for us that works with frozen blueberries no problem and is perfectly accompanied by a great cup of coffee.

NOTE: THIS RECIPE WORKS EQUALLY WELL AS A LOAF YOU CAN SLICE, OR AS A STREUSEL COFFEE CAKE YOU CAN CUT INTO SQUARES. CHOOSE YOUR PAN ACCORDINGLY.

YOU WILL NEED

- 9-x-5-inch loaf pan or one 9-inch square pan, lightly greased with nonstick cooking spray, and lined with parchment paper (leave about 2 inches of excess paper on two sides to act as "handles" to remove the cake from the pan before cutting and serving)

INGREDIENTS

BLUEBERRY CAKE

- 1 cup (150 g) fresh blueberries or frozen blueberries, thawed and drained
- 1¾ cups (275 g) + 1 to 2 tablespoons all-purpose flour
- ½ cup (125 ml) avocado or olive oil
- ¼ cup (60 ml) orange juice
- ¼ cup (60 ml) lemon juice
- 1 cup (200 g) granulated sugar
- 2 large eggs
- ½ cup (125 ml) crème fraîche
- 1 teaspoon vanilla extract
- Zest of 1 lemon
- 1 teaspoon baking soda
- 1 teaspoon salt

STREUSEL TOPPING

- ¼ cup (40 g) all-purpose flour
- 2 tablespoons granulated sugar
- 2 tablespoons light brown sugar
- ½ teaspoon ground cinnamon
- ⅛ teaspoon salt
- 2 tablespoons unsalted butter, cut into ½-inch cubes

DIRECTIONS

Preheat the oven to 350°F.

Toss the blueberries in 1 to 2 tablespoons of the flour until coated; this will prevent them from sinking in the batter as the cake bakes. Set aside.

Make the streusel topping
Combine the flour, granulated sugar, brown sugar, cinnamon, and salt in a bowl. Using your fingertips, rub the butter into the flour mixture until evenly distributed and the mixture is crumbly. Refrigerate until ready to use.

Make the cake
In a large mixing bowl, whisk the oil, orange and lemon juices, and sugar until the mixture is bright yellow and the sugar has started to dissolve. Add the eggs, crème fraîche, vanilla, and lemon zest, whisking until completely smooth.

In a separate bowl, whisk together the remaining flour, baking soda, and salt. Gradually add the flour mixture to the batter, stirring gently. Gently fold in the blueberries until evenly distributed.

Transfer the batter to the prepared pan, using a spatula to spread it evenly in the pan and smooth the surface. Use your fingers to distribute the streusel topping evenly over the batter, breaking up any large clumps. Bake until the cake is golden brown, and a toothpick or cake tester inserted into the center comes out clean, about 55 minutes.

Remove from the oven and transfer to a wire rack to cool for 20 to 30 minutes before lifting the cake out of the pan and cutting it into squares to serve.

Serve with vanilla ice cream, and remind yourself that summer will one day, eventually, return. If not enjoying immediately, this cake will keep refrigerated in an airtight container for up to 5 days.

Earl Grey Pound Cake

◦ MAKES ONE 9-INCH LOAF (SERVES 8) ◦

MANDY | Nothing reminds me more of my mom and her mom (Nana, of "chew" fame; see page 212) than Twinings Earl Grey tea. When we were little, we would be allowed to share a pot of tea with them. She taught us—in what we think is proper British form—how to "hot the pot" and that a perfect cup of tea could be enjoyed with brown sugar cubes and a splash of cream. Often, we would sip the tea while enjoying shortbread, Social Tea biscuits, scones, or some other buttery treat. And so what better way to remember Nana than to infuse the bergamot deliciousness of Earl Grey into a classic pound cake! To this day, I still enjoy a mug of sweetened Earl Grey tea every night before bed.

YOU WILL NEED

- 9-x -5-inch loaf pan, lightly greased with nonstick cooking spray and dusted with flour

INGREDIENTS

EARL GREY POUND CAKE

- 1 cup (225 g) unsalted butter, softened
- 1⅓ cups (275 g) granulated sugar
- 2 tablespoons loose-leaf Earl Grey
- 5 large eggs
- 1 teaspoon vanilla extract
- 2 cups (320 g) all-purpose flour
- 1 teaspoon salt

CREAM GLAZE

- 2 cups (200 g) confectioners' sugar
- 7 to 8 tablespoons (105 to 120 ml) heavy cream, or more as needed

DIRECTIONS

Make the cake
Preheat the oven to 350°F.

Using a stand mixer fitted with the paddle attachment, cream the butter, sugar, and tea leaves on medium speed until the mixture is light and fluffy and the scent of the tea leaves starts to emerge, 3 to 4 minutes. Add the eggs one at a time, mixing on medium speed until incorporated, about 20 seconds each. Scrape down the sides of the bowl as needed after each egg has been added. Add the vanilla.

In a separate bowl, whisk together the flour and salt. Add to the bowl of the stand mixer and mix on low speed until the tea leaves are evenly distributed, about 30 seconds.

Pour the batter into the prepared pan, using a spatula to spread in an even layer. Bake until the surface of the cake is golden and a toothpick or cake tester inserted into the thickest part comes out clean, 55 to 60 minutes.

Remove from the oven and let cool in the pan for 10 minutes, then unmold onto a wire rack to cool completely.

Make the glaze
Whisk the confectioners' sugar and cream together in a bowl to form a thick glaze—if it's too thin, add a bit more confectioners' sugar; if it's too thick, add a little more cream. Spoon the glaze over the top of the loaf, letting it drip generously down the sides. Let the glaze set for 10 minutes before transferring to a serving platter and slicing. This cake will keep refrigerated in an airtight container for up to 5 days.

Lazy Pumpkin Pies

◦ MAKES TWO 9-INCH PIES (SERVES 6 TO 8 EACH) ◦

Our parents' best friends, dating back to when they all were in their teens and early 20s, have always been Joe and Cathy Hiess. As a result, we Wolfe kids grew up alongside the two Hiess boys, and in the last decade we have made it a point to see each other over the holidays as we watch our own kids grow up now too. The Hiesses, like us, celebrate both Christmas and Hanukkah, as well as our favorite holiday, Thanksgiving. We celebrate Thanksgiving with them up in the Laurentians every October (in Canada, anyway!), which also happens to be around Joodles's, Joe's, and Cathy's birthdays too. A must-have classic dessert at this time of year is pumpkin pie. Here's our family's favorite, and the recipe makes two pies—crucial for large gatherings. Little secret: we totally cheat with this one and use some good old Tenderflake pastry dough from the grocery store freezer aisle: works like a charm, keeps the focus on the pumpkin spice flavors, and saves you tons of time.

INGREDIENTS

- 2 9-inch frozen pie shells
- 2 cups (500 ml) pumpkin puree
- 3 large eggs
- 1¼ cups (240 g) firmly packed brown sugar
- 1 tablespoon cornstarch
- ½ teaspoon salt
- 1½ teaspoons ground cinnamon
- ½ teaspoon ground ginger
- ¼ teaspoon ground nutmeg
- ⅛ teaspoon ground cloves
- ⅛ teaspoon freshly ground black pepper
- 1 cup (250 ml) heavy cream
- ¼ cup (60 ml) whole milk
- 1 egg yolk, beaten with 1 tablespoon milk or cream, for egg wash

DIRECTIONS

Preheat the oven to 375°F. Place the frozen pie shells on a large sheet tray.

In a large bowl, whisk the pumpkin puree, eggs, and brown sugar together until smooth and thoroughly combined. Add the cornstarch, salt, cinnamon, ginger, nutmeg, cloves, pepper, cream, and milk, whisking vigorously to combine.

Pour equal amounts of pie filling into each pie crust. Brush the rim of each pie shell with the egg wash. Bake the pies until their centers are almost set, about 50 minutes. Part of the center will look wobbly, but that's okay. The pies will set as they cool.

Allow to cool to room temperature on a wire rack, 2 to 3 hours, before cutting into wedges and serving. These pies will keep, refrigerated, for up to 5 days.

Mini Peanut Butter and Chocolate Fondants

∘ MAKES 8 MINI (INDIVIDUAL) CAKES ∘

MANDY | One of my all-time favorite dessert combinations is indubitably chocolate and peanut butter. I came across a Donna Hay recipe for a molten PB and chocolate cake a few years ago and riffed on it to create a saltier and more textured dessert, using chunky peanut butter instead of creamy—it's delicious either way! To celebrate the opening of our Crescent Street location in 2015, we made a ton of small fondant cakes for the team to enjoy after slinging hundreds of salads. They will always taste of satisfaction to me. And, of course, who doesn't love having a miniature confection to themselves?

NOTE: WE LOVE VALRHONA FOR ALL THEIR CHOCOLATE PRODUCTS, BUT IF YOU CAN'T FIND VALRHONA EASILY, AIM FOR THE BEST-QUALITY CHOCOLATE YOU CAN FIND TO ACHIEVE RICH CHOCOLATY FLAVOR. I USUALLY MAKE THIS RECIPE WITH JIF EXTRA CRUNCHY PEANUT BUTTER.

YOU WILL NEED

∘ 12-cup muffin pan with ½-cup inserts, 8 of the inserts lightly greased with nonstick cooking spray and dusted with flour

INGREDIENTS

∘ 1½ cups (200 g) dark chocolate pastilles or chopped dark chocolate, plus extra for topping (optional)
∘ 7 tablespoons (100 g) salted butter, cut into ½-inch cubes
∘ 2 large eggs
∘ 2 egg yolks
∘ ½ cup (100 g) granulated sugar
∘ ½ teaspoon Maldon salt
∘ ¼ cup (40 g) all-purpose flour
∘ ½ cup (125 ml) chunky peanut butter
∘ 2 tablespoons each cocoa powder and ground cinnamon, combined, for dusting

DIRECTIONS

Preheat the oven to 400°F.

In a small, heavy-bottomed saucepan, over medium-low heat, melt the chocolate and butter, whisking occasionally to combine until smooth. (You can also melt the chocolate and butter in a bowl in the microwave, in two blasts of 30 seconds each, stirring the mixture after each round.)

In a large bowl, whisk the eggs, egg yolks, sugar, and salt vigorously until pale in color. Whisk in the chocolate-butter mixture, followed by the flour, and mix until smooth.

Scoop approximately 2 tablespoons of the chocolate batter into each of the 8 prepared cups in the muffin pan. Next, spoon 1 tablespoon of peanut butter onto the center of each, followed by another tablespoon of the chocolate batter. Use the back of a spoon or your (clean) fingers to smooth the chocolate over the top to cover the peanut butter completely. Press extra chocolate chunks into each if you like it extra chocolaty.

Bake for 14 to 16 minutes, until puffed. Use a small offset spatula and a spoon to gently scoop out each mini cake onto a serving platter or individual plates, and dust with the cocoa and cinnamon powder to serve. Enjoy immediately for the full melty-center effect—though these are still great once cooled completely! They will keep refrigerated in an airtight container for up to 3 days.

Chai Tea Cake with Salted Caramel Glaze

∘ MAKES ONE 10-INCH BUNDT CAKE (SERVES 8 TO 10) ∘

We don't know exactly when the chai tea blend became the new mid-afternoon flavor latte or the pick-me-up hot beverage (sometime in the 90s?), but we're guessing it became popular here after all the yogis came back from trips to India. It always has me feeling all things autumn, pumpkin spice, and just downright cozy. So why not enjoy it in edible form?! This elegant Bundt hits all the chai notes—cinnamon, cardamom, ginger, and clove. And we use tea leaves to get there, but also underline their rich flavor with fresh spices.

YOU WILL NEED

∘ 10-inch Bundt pan, lightly greased with nonstick cooking spray

INGREDIENTS

∘ 1 tablespoon loose-leaf chai tea leaves
∘ 2½ cups (375 g) all-purpose flour
∘ 3 teaspoons baking powder
∘ ½ teaspoon baking soda
∘ 1 teaspoon salt
∘ 1½ cups (300 g) granulated sugar
∘ ½ teaspoon ground nutmeg
∘ ½ teaspoon ground cinnamon
∘ ½ teaspoon ground allspice
∘ ½ teaspoon ground ginger
∘ 4 large eggs
∘ 1½ cups (375 ml) whole milk
∘ ½ cup (125 ml) sour cream or crème fraîche
∘ 1 cup (225 g) salted butter, melted
∘ 2 teaspoons vanilla extract
∘ 1 recipe Salted Caramel Glaze (page 221)

DIRECTIONS

Preheat the oven to 350°F.

In a small bowl or cup, combine the tea leaves with 2 tablespoons of boiling water and stir. Set aside.

In a large bowl, whisk the flour, baking powder, baking soda, salt, sugar, nutmeg, cinnamon, allspice, and ginger to combine.

In a separate bowl, whisk together the steeped tea leaves, eggs, milk, sour cream, melted butter, and vanilla until smooth.

Whisk the wet mixture into the dry mixture until just combined.

Pour the mixture into a 10-inch Bundt pan and cook for 35 to 40 minutes, until a toothpick or cake tester inserted into the center comes out clean. While the cake is baking, make the salted caramel glaze.

Remove the cake from the oven and allow to cool in the pan for 10 minutes, then use an offset spatula to loosen the cake at the edges and around the inner tube and invert it onto a wire rack.

Transfer the cake to a serving platter, then spoon the warm caramel glaze over the cake, letting it drip down the sides. Allow the glaze to set for at least 10 minutes before slicing and serving.

This tea cake will keep in an airtight container at room temperature for up to 3 days.

Toblerone Oatmeal Squares

∘ MAKES 16 SQUARES ∘

Our mom, Joodles, hits it out of the park with this classic Wolfe dessert: it reminds us entirely of our childhood and of our late father, Jason, who would have dessert after every meal if he could. Sometimes he actually did: when we were up north at the cottage on weekends, he'd polish off cinnamon rolls for lunch, having just enjoyed eggs, bacon, and buttery croissants for breakfast. His sweet tooth was legendary, and we can confidently say it's most definitely genetic.

YOU WILL NEED

∘ 8-inch square baking pan, lightly greased with nonstick cooking spray and lined with parchment paper (leave about 2 inches of excess paper on two sides to act as "handles" to remove the slab from the pan before cutting and serving)

INGREDIENTS

∘ ½ cup (113 g) salted butter, cut into ½-inch cubes + 1 tablespoon
∘ ¼ cup (50 g) granulated sugar
∘ ¼ cup (40 g) lightly packed light brown sugar
∘ 1 (large) egg yolk
∘ ½ teaspoon vanilla extract
∘ ½ cup (80 g) all-purpose flour
∘ ½ cup (50 g) rolled oats
∘ 1 cup (200 g) chopped Toblerone milk chocolate

DIRECTIONS

Preheat the oven to 350°F.

Place the cubed butter (leaving the additional tablespoon aside), granulated sugar, brown sugar, egg yolk, and vanilla in the bowl of your food processor (fitted with the metal blade) and pulse five times, then process for 30 seconds until the mixture is uniform. Add the flour and process for 4 to 5 seconds to combine. Add the oats next and pulse quickly 3 to 4 times to incorporate—you don't want to turn the oats to mush!

Spread the mixture into the prepared baking pan. Bake for 20 to 25 minutes, until golden and browning around the edges. Let cool completely in the pan, placed on a wire rack.

Melt the chocolate and the remaining 1 tablespoon of butter in a bowl in the microwave, in blasts of 30 seconds each, stirring the mixture after each round, until smooth and completely melted.

Pour the melted chocolate evenly over the oatmeal base and smooth with an offset spatula. Let cool completely at room temperature. Use the parchment paper overhang to lift the slab out of the pan and transfer to a cutting board. Cut into 16 2-inch squares.

Enjoy with a nice tall glass of cold Québon milk as our dad would have . . . or oat, hemp, almond, or macadamia milks work too!

These squares will keep for up to 7 days in an airtight container at room temperature.

Nana's "Chew"

Every Wednesday night, our mom's mom, Nana as she was known, would come over for dinner. She and my mom would break out the bottle of Harveys Bristol Cream sherry, and ancient stories would be told, as well as new memories made. Nana never came over without a dessert in hand, one of which was what she called her "chew"—the name made perfect sense to us, as it was chewy and gooey, and we loved every bite. So, what is it? Remember those favorite oatmeal raisin cookies that you loved as a kid? That familiar chewiness and texture of the oats? Our Nana turned that nostalgic flavor into a square baked brownie of sorts, swapping out the chocolate for juicy raisins and adding an extra sweetness and tropical twist with shredded coconut.

YOU WILL NEED

- 8-inch square baking pan, lightly greased with nonstick cooking spray and lined with parchment paper (leave about 2 inches of excess paper on two sides to act as "handles" to remove the slab from the pan before cutting and serving)

INGREDIENTS

- 1 cup (215 g) firmly packed light brown sugar
- ¾ cup (100 g) all-purpose flour
- 1 teaspoon baking powder
- ¼ cup (57 g) salted butter, melted
- 1 large egg, beaten
- ½ cup (45 g) unsweetened shredded coconut
- ½ cup (90 g) sultanas (golden raisins)

DIRECTIONS

Preheat the oven to 350°F.

In a mixing bowl, combine the sugar, flour, and baking powder. Using a wooden spoon or spatula, stir in the melted butter and egg until combined, then stir in the shredded coconut and sultanas until evenly distributed.

Transfer the thick batter to the prepared pan and spread it out into a thin, even layer using an offset spatula or the back of a spoon. Bake for 15 minutes until set and golden brown around the edges. Let cool completely in the pan, placed on a wire rack.

Use the parchment paper overhang to transfer the slab to a cutting board, and cut into 16 2-inch squares to serve.

These chews will keep for up to 5 days in an airtight container at room temperature.

Fudge for All

∘ ONE 8-INCH SQUARE PAN'S WORTH (16 TO 32 PIECES) ∘

MANDY | **Every summer we decamp to Kennebunkport, Maine, with the ever-growing Wolfe family. One of our favorite Maine traditions has to be going into the local candy shops, filling our bags with dentist-feared amounts of sweets, saltwater taffies, and, of course, fudge. As I write this, I can clearly see the small waxy white cardboard boxes with their picturesque lighthouses! Inside one of them lies our all-time favorite: tiny squares of creamy sweet fudge. Making fudge is a lot easier than you might think (you just need to allow time for it to set), and we like adding toasted walnuts to ours! (PS: We know this book is mainly about autumn and winter, but we forgot to include this must-have recipe in our first book, and you haaaave to have it!)**

YOU WILL NEED

- Instant-read digital thermometer or candy thermometer
- 8-inch square baking pan, lightly greased with nonstick cooking spray and lined with parchment paper (leave about 2 inches of excess paper on two sides to act as "handles" to remove the fudge from the pan before cutting and serving)

INGREDIENTS

- 2¾ cups (454 g) lightly packed light brown sugar
- 1½ cups (375 ml) evaporated milk
- ½ cup (113 g) butter, cut into ½-inch cubes
- ½ teaspoon vanilla
- ½ cup (60 g) walnuts, toasted and coarsely chopped

DIRECTIONS

In a heavy-bottomed saucepan over medium-low heat, bring the sugar, evaporated milk, and butter to a rolling boil, whisking regularly. Continue to cook, while still boiling, for 8 to 10 minutes, to get the fudge to the "soft ball" stage, in the range of 235°F to 237°F. (If you don't have a thermometer, you can determine the soft ball stage by dropping a small spoonful of the fudge syrup into a glass of cold water. Let the dropped fudge cool for a second, then try to form it into a small ball with your fingers. If it holds its shape but still feels soft, you've reached the soft ball stage!)

Remove the pan from the heat and keep whisking the fudge for 2 to 3 minutes. Stir in the vanilla and walnuts, then pour into the prepared pan. Refrigerate until set, at least 2 hours or overnight.

Use the parchment paper overhang to transfer the fudge to a cutting board, and cut into the size of your choice (potentially 32 small rectangles or 16 2-inch squares).

This fudge will keep for up to 2 weeks in an airtight container at room temperature.

Passover Matzo Brittle

∘ MAKES ONE 10-INCH DIAMETER COOKIE TIN'S WORTH (SERVES 6) ∘

Passover is a festive time of year for us "members of the tribe," a time of year when Jewish classics and revamped versions of heritage dishes get made, shared, and consumed at alarming rates. One of our absolute favorite things to make is this matzo toffee brittle, which is just a very simple and clever way to jazz up matzo with buttery brown sugar caramel, melted chocolate, and some toasted nuts. It's sweet, salty, chocolaty, and absolutely addictive, and it reminds us a little (okay, a lot) of Skor bars! Jewish or not, you'll be hooked. Note from our tester Kendra: "I couldn't stop eating it; I shared it with no one."

NOTE: WE LOVE TO TOP THIS WITH NUTS FOR SOME ADDED CRUNCH, BUT YOU COULD PLAY WITH ANY NUMBER OF ALTERNATIVES: MALDON SALT, SOME DRIED OR CANDIED FRUIT CUT UP SMALL, OR EVEN CRUMBLED SALTY POTATO CHIPS!

YOU WILL NEED

- Parchment-lined 13- x 9-inch sheet tray

INGREDIENTS

- 5 sheets classic plain matzos
- 1 cup (225 g) salted butter
- 1 cup (175 g) lightly packed light brown sugar
- 2 cups (350 g) semi-sweet chocolate chips
- 1 teaspoon Maldon salt
- 1 cup (140 g) coarsely chopped almond slivers or pecans

DIRECTIONS

Preheat the oven to 350°F.

Cover the entire surface of the parchment paper with the matzos; you'll have to break the crackers to make them fit nicely next to each other. (It's okay to have them slightly overlapping.) Set aside.

In a heavy-bottomed saucepan over medium-high heat, whisk the butter and brown sugar until a smooth caramel sauce starts to form. Boil for 3 to 4 minutes, whisking often, until the sauce begins to thicken. Pour the sauce over the matzos and, using an offset spatula, spread it over every possible inch of cracker. The sauce may seep through the holes in the matzos, and that's completely okay!

Bake for 8 to 10 minutes, until the caramel is bubbling evenly and golden brown all over.

Remove from the oven and sprinkle the chocolate chips all over the hot caramel matzos. Return to the oven for 90 seconds. Remove from the oven again and spread the melted chocolate chips evenly over the caramel using an offset spatula. Sprinkle with the Maldon salt, followed by the chopped nuts (or the toppings of your choice).

Freeze for at least 1 hour, or even overnight. Use a chef's knife to break the matzo brittle into pieces of your preferred size and shape before serving. The brittle will keep in an airtight container for all 8 days of Passover, but you may want to double the recipe if you intend to keep it that long!

Joodles's Birthday Cupcakes

° MAKES ABOUT 18 CUPCAKES °

Growing up in a relatively big family, we became accustomed to meals and desserts being made in a kind of homemade Costco-size quantity, constantly. There was never ONE pizza, or ONE bag of six bagels in our house, or two bananas, it was always army-canteen style. When it was one of our birthdays, our mom would make not one dozen cupcakes, she would make five dozen. At Mandy's, we love celebrating birthdays too, and these recipes have come in very handy for our 300+ employees.

INGREDIENTS

Two 12-cup muffin pans or
three 6-cup muffin pans,
lined with paper liners

INGREDIENTS

- 1¾ cups (275 g) all-purpose flour
- 1 cup (200 g) granulated sugar
- ¼ teaspoon baking soda
- 1½ teaspoons baking powder
- ¼ teaspoon salt
- ¾ cup (170 g) salted
  butter, melted
- 3 large eggs, at room
  temperature
- ½ cup (125 ml) sour cream
- ½ cup (125 ml) whole milk
- 1 tablespoon vanilla extract
- 1 recipe Cupcake
  Frosting (see below)
- 1 cup (200 g) Smarties

DIRECTIONS

Preheat the oven to 350°F.

In a large bowl, add the flour, sugar, baking soda, baking powder, and salt and whisk to combine. Set aside.

In another bowl, whisk together the melted butter, eggs, sour cream, milk, and vanilla until thoroughly combined and smooth.

Use a spatula to mix the flour mixture gently into the wet batter until just combined.

Use a cookie scoop to distribute the batter evenly into the cupcake papers, filling each paper no more than two-thirds full (you should get about 18 cupcakes, or if you err on the side of caution, you will end up with more).

Bake, with the muffin tins side by side on the middle rack, for about 18 minutes, until the cupcakes have domed up and are a little firm to the touch but still pale, and a toothpick inserted into the center comes out clean.

Remove from the oven and let the cupcakes cool in the pan for 10 minutes, then transfer to a wire rack and let cool completely before frosting, about 1 hour.

If you're going for a handmade look, use a spoon or small offset spatula to frost each cupcake. If you want to get fancy, you can also pipe the frosting—break out the decorating tools or simply use a ziplock bag with a corner cut off. Add as many Smarties to each cupcake as you like, pressing each one gently into the frosting. Happy birthday! If not using immediately, transfer to an airtight container and refrigerate for up to 5 days.

CUPCAKE FROSTING

MAKES 3 CUPS

INGREDIENTS

- 1 cup (225 g) salted butter,
  at room temperature
- 4 cups (450 g)
  confectioners' sugar
- 1 teaspoon vanilla extract
- 1 tablespoon heavy cream
- 1 teaspoon whole milk
- 1 pinch salt

DIRECTIONS

Using a stand mixer fitted with the paddle attachment, cream the butter until light and fluffy, about 1 minute at medium speed. Stop the mixer and add half of the confectioners' sugar. Resume beating to incorporate, then stop the mixer and add the remaining confectioners' sugar and beat until fluffy once more. Add the vanilla, cream, milk, and salt and mix until completely incorporated.

Salted Caramel Pecan Brownies

◦ MAKES 16 BROWNIES ◦

Aside from our chocolate chip cookies (recipe in our first book), these brownies are our biggest dessert seller. The base is dense and moist, and super decadent on its own. Add the luscious, melty salted caramel sauce on top, plus crunchy pecans, and you can see how they sell out most lunchtimes.

NOTE: WE LOVE VALRHONA FOR ALL THEIR CHOCOLATE PRODUCTS, BUT IF YOU CAN'T FIND VALRHONA, AIM FOR THE BEST-QUALITY DUTCH-PROCESS COCOA POWDER AND CHOCOLATE CHIPS YOU CAN FIND TO ACHIEVE RICH CHOCOLATY FLAVOR—GHIRARDELLI IS GREAT TOO!

YOU WILL NEED

- 8-inch square cake pan, lightly greased with nonstick cooking spray, and lined with parchment paper (leave about 2 inches of excess paper on two sides to act as "handles" to remove the brownie from the pan before cutting and serving)

INGREDIENTS

- 1½ cups (300 g) granulated sugar
- 3 large eggs
- ¾ cup (170 g) salted butter, melted, cooled
- 2 teaspoons vanilla extract
- ¾ cup (100 g) all-purpose flour
- ¾ cup (85 g) unsweetened cocoa powder
- ¾ cup (150 g) semi-sweet chocolate chips
- 1 recipe Salted Caramel Glaze (see below)
- 1 cup (100 g) pecans, toasted, coarsely chopped
- Maldon salt, for sprinkling

DIRECTIONS

Preheat the oven to 300°F.

In a large mixing bowl, whisk together the sugar and eggs until well combined, then stir in the melted butter and vanilla.

In a small bowl, whisk together the flour and cocoa powder before stirring it into the butter mixture until just combined. Using a wooden spoon or spatula, fold in the chocolate chips, stirring only until evenly distributed.

Transfer the thick batter to the prepared pan and spread it out in an even layer with your wooden spoon or a spatula. Bake until set and barely firm in the middle (it's okay if your toothpick or cake tester shows a hint of sticky batter when inserted into the center), 35 to 40 minutes. Remove from the oven and let cool completely on a wire rack.

Pour the salted caramel glaze evenly over the brownie base and smooth it out with an offset spatula. Sprinkle with the chopped pecans and a couple of pinches of Maldon salt flakes.

If you're in a rush to enjoy these brownies, refrigerate until the caramel starts to set, 1 to 2 hours. Otherwise, let cool completely at room temperature. When cool and the caramel has set, use the parchment paper overhang to transfer to a cutting board. Cut into 16 2-inch squares.

These brownies will keep for up to 4 days in an airtight container at room temperature.

SALTED CARAMEL GLAZE

MAKES 1 CUP

INGREDIENTS

- 1 cup (200 g) granulated sugar
- 6 tablespoons (85 g) salted butter, cut into ½-inch cubes
- ½ cup (125 ml) heavy cream, at room temperature
- 1 teaspoon salt

DIRECTIONS

Add ¼ cup of water to a small heavy-bottomed saucepan over medium heat, and sprinkle the sugar into the center of the saucepan—do not stir it in. Bring to a simmer and the sugar will eventually melt into the water. Simmer, undisturbed, until the sugar syrup begins to turn a deep amber color, 7 to 9 minutes. Swirl the pot gently once or twice at this point to even the caramel out.

Reduce the heat to the lowest possible setting and whisk in the butter gently but quickly (take care: the water content of the butter will cause the caramel to sputter and steam!), continuing to cook the caramel mixture for about 2 minutes, swirling the pan occasionally. Very slowly drizzle in the cream while stirring continuously. Allow the mixture to boil for a minute or so (it will bubble up in the saucepan as it cooks). Remove from the heat and stir in 1 teaspoon of salt (or more, to taste).

This caramel sauce will keep, refrigerated, in an airtight container for up to 1 month or frozen for up to 3 months. Gently warm the sauce to loosen it before using.

Crew Love

Acknowledgments

We have come through an extraordinary time in not just our business, but in our city, our country, and our entire world. Writing a second cookbook during a global pandemic is not something we ever thought we would be doing.

To the fans and supporters who showed us so much love when our first book came out in July 2020—thank you so much. It filled our hearts with such encouragement, and we were honored to see you sharing photos and clips of you making salads at home in quarantine, during curfews, and in lockdowns.

To our BTS invisible crew who worked tirelessly and incredibly hard to get this second book out to you all: Lachlan McGillivray for his extraordinary planning, food prep, and patience during our epic photo shoots; Kendra McKnight for recipe testing and honest feedback; Sarah Lazar and her team for all the sensational design; Alison Slattery for these incredible photos; and Meredith for co-writing this book like the new-mom champ she is halfway around the world. Thank you also to everyone at Penguin Random House Canada who worked behind the scenes, and have always been such big fans and so easy to work with. And thank you to all the retailers who supported our first book.

Finally and ultimately, thank you to everyone who works with us at our restaurants. This book is an ode to you, our very own frontline workers: our managers, salad artists, chefs, ambassadors, team captains, buddies, trainers, dishwashers, and catering team. And to our teams in finance, external sales, branding and marketing, operations, supply chain management, HR, DM, and our CFO. Each and every one of you has contributed to the growth and success of our family-run company—you have all helped make this humble dream come true and we could not be more grateful.

This book is for you: our whacky, funny, OG extended work family.

Big love and gratitude always,

Mandy and Rebecca

Index

MANDY and **REBECCA WOLFE** are the co-authors of the bestselling cookbook Mandy's Gourmet Salads, and owners of the salad bars of the same name. Mandy is the creative food director and chef, while Rebecca designs all locations and heads brand marketing. Together, they also founded the Welcome Collective, a charitable organization that welcomes refugee claimants to Canada. When they're not making salads, they can be found raising their seven vegetable-loving kids in the heart of Montreal.

⬡ mandysalads

MEREDITH ERICKSON is the author of *Alpine Cooking*. She has co-authored *The Art of Living According to Joe Beef, Le Pigeon, Olympia Provisions, Kristen Kish Cooking, Claridge's: The Cookbook, Joe Beef: Surviving the Apocalypse, Friuli Food and Wine*, and the Canadian bestseller *Mandy's Gourmet Salads*. She is the host of the Audible original series *Field Guide to Eating in Canada*. Meredith splits her time between Montreal and Milan.

⬡ ericksonmeredith

ALISON SLATTERY is a Montreal-based food photographer hailing from Southwest Ireland. Her photography has appeared in *Condé Nast Traveler, The New York Times, Food & Wine, enRoute, Caribou*, and *Tastet*, as well books like, *True North*, and *Mandy's Gourmet Salads*. Alison can also be found on one of Montreal's most iconic Instagram food photography feeds.

⬡ twofoodphotographers

SARAH LAZAR is the founder of graphic design studio Cow Goes Moo. Specializing in brand development, her team has had the opportunity to work with clients in industries from healthcare and wellness, to Montreal's bustling restaurant scene. Her studio's collaboration with Mandy's (one of their very first clients) began in 2006. When they're not at their computers, Sarah and her team can be found printing all things Letterpress.

⬡ cowgoesmoo   ⬡ wegomoo